The wonder, depth, and reality of the "hope" God's plan and purpose intended for each individual human being is an unshakeable truth revealed in the Bible. Jonathan Bernis is an able teacher, a schooled rabbi, and a prolific author whose writings have assisted multitudes toward biblical and theological clarity on practical issues. I believe he will offer much to profit any reader who will earnestly open to the foundational truth and helpful insights he offers here.

—JACK W. HAYFORD
CHANCELLOR, THE KING'S UNIVERSITY
PASTOR EMERITUS, THE CHURCH ON THE WAY

Have you ever questioned why you're here? Do you wonder what God's plan is for you? If so, I highly recommend you read *A Hope and a Future* by Jonathan Bernis, one of the strongest voices in the Messianic Jewish church. In it he explains how God's promises are still true today, and He has a plan for your life. I believe this book will be a great encouragement to you as you find hope and peace in the knowledge that your future is safe in His hands.

—ROBERT MORRIS
FOUNDING SENIOR PASTOR, GATEWAY CHURCH
DALLAS/FORT WORTH, TEXAS
BEST-SELLING AUTHOR, *THE BLESSED LIFE, FROM DREAM TO DESTINY, THE GOD I NEVER KNEW, AND TRULY FREE*

Wherever I go, I see fear, doom, and gloom, even among some of God's people. Many are preparing for hard times by storing up food, water, and shotguns, 　　　　　　　　 'ing you. But you must not allow 　　　　　　　　 d's plan for your destiny. You mu 　　　　　　　　

A Hope and a Future, the 　　　　　　　　 ian Bernis, is just what the doctor ordered. 　　　 .ope

D1279993

vaccine to be "normal"—normal as defined by the Bible. Step up and get your shot of hope. It's painless!

—SID ROTH
HOST, *IT'S SUPERNATURAL!*

Words of encouragement, hope, and faith from a reliable source, Messianic Jewish leader Jonathan Bernis. In these uncertain and chaotic times, this book will ground you in God's Word and help you to take hold of His good purposes for your life.

—DR. MICHAEL L. BROWN
PRESIDENT, FIRE SCHOOL OF MINISTRY
AUTHOR, *ANSWERING JEWISH OBJECTIONS TO JESUS.*

I wholeheartedly endorse Jonathan's new book *A Hope and a Future*! This is the kind of book everyone is yearning for. Too often in our lives we wonder where God went without realizing He has never left. We left Him! He is wooing us back as each of us are children of destiny. He placed your life in history when He needed someone just like you for a mission only you could fulfill! When Israel was going through its worst time in history, with the temple being destroyed, the Jewish people taken into captivity, Jeremiah penned those words that God still has a hope and a future for them. He also has one for you! Return to Him and call upon the name of the Lord and see what great things He has in store for you! This book will be a great encouragement!

—PASTOR MARK BILTZ

A
HOPE
AND A
FUTURE

A HOPE
AND A
FUTURE

JONATHAN BERNIS

CHARISMA
HOUSE

A HOPE AND A FUTURE by Jonathan Bernis
Published by Charisma House
Charisma Media/Charisma House Book Group
600 Rinehart Road
Lake Mary, Florida 32746
www.charismahouse.com

Scripture quotations marked NKJV are taken from the New King James Version®. Copyright © 1982 by Thomas Nelson. Used by permission. All rights reserved.

Scripture quotations marked THE MESSAGE are from *The Message: The Bible in Contemporary English,* copyright © 1993, 1994, 1995, 1996, 2000, 2001, 2002. Used by permission of NavPress Publishing Group.

Cover design by Justin Evans

Visit the author's website at www.jewishvoice.org.

Library of Congress Cataloging-in-Publication Data:
An application to register this book for cataloging has been submitted to the Library of Congress.
International Standard Book Number: 978-1-62998-654-8 (trade paper); ISBN: 978-1-62998-955-6 (hardback)
E-book ISBN: 978-1-62998-655-5

While the author has made every effort to provide accurate Internet addresses at the time of publication, neither the publisher nor the author assumes any responsibility for errors or for changes that occur after publication.

First edition

16 17 18 19 20 — 987654321
Printed in the United States of America

CONTENTS

Chapter 1

GOD HAS A
PLAN FOR YOU

*Your eyes saw me when I was unformed, and
in Your book were written the days that were
formed—when not one of them had come to be.*

—Psalm 139:16

DO YOU EVER feel like our world is spinning out of control? We turn on the news and see the horrors unleashed by groups like ISIS in the Middle East and Boko Haram in Africa. Even here in the United States we live with the constant threat of terrorism. Some say that if terrorists don't destroy us, global warming very well might.

The future seems so uncertain. One day the stock market is up. The next day it's down. The economy seems to be going in the right direction, and then the "experts" say we're on the verge of another recession or imminent economic collapse. Politicians are talking about overhauling Social Security and Medicare. Will those programs even be there for us when we really need them? And I haven't even mentioned crime, disease, or unexpected tragedies like car crashes that impact thousands of lives every day.

Here we are, clinging to a tiny planet whipping through space at over one thousand miles an hour. And yet, in the midst of this seemingly uncertain world, we are held safely in the arms of a God who never changes—who is the same yesterday, today, and forever (Heb. 13:8).

This is wonderful news. God has a plan for the earth as a whole, *and* He has a plan for every individual human being who lives here. That includes you.

GOD IS IN CONTROL

God is not the least bit surprised by any of the problems we are facing. Two thousand years ago, the Messiah Yeshua (Jesus) warned that there would be wars and rumors of wars, that nation would rise against nation and there would be earthquakes and famines. He also gave us these comforting words to cling to: "In the world you will have trouble. But take heart! I have overcome the world." (John 16:33, NIV).

One of my favorite Bible passages is this priceless gem from Jeremiah 29:11–14 (NIV):

> "For I know the plans I have for you," declares the LORD, "plans to prosper you and not to harm you, plans to give you hope and a future. Then you will call on me and come and pray to me, and I will listen to you. You will seek me and find me when you seek me with all your heart. I will be found by you," declares the LORD, "and will bring you back from captivity. I will gather you from all the nations and places where I have banished you," declares the LORD, "and will bring you back to the place from which I carried you into exile."

This prophecy was given to the Jewish people by the prophet Jeremiah over twenty-five hundred years ago. Today, these words are being fulfilled as Jewish men, women, and children are returning to the restored land of Israel from nations around the earth.

But even though these words were spoken to a nation of people over twenty-five hundred years ago, I believe they also apply to every one of us, to every individual who is a child of God. The Bible refers to the Jews as God's chosen people. Whether you are a Jew who has come to faith in the Messiah as I have, or a Gentile (a non-Jew) who has come to that same faith in Yeshua HaMashiach (Jesus Christ), you are a child of God, and His promise belongs to you, too.

I am writing this book because I want to give you a full understanding of how one incredible verse—Jeremiah 29:11— applies to you and those you love. These are important words that require reflection, study, and even action on our part.

It's not enough to read these comforting words, think "What a beautiful passage," and move on. This message from God can be life changing! Only when we dig deeper, find the true meaning of what God is saying here, and apply it to our lives will we receive what our heavenly Father desires to give us.

God Had a Plan for My Life

I am proof positive that God has a plan for all of us—and that plan is not necessarily what I would have chosen for myself. In fact, it's much better. Otherwise, I would never be doing what I'm doing today.

I was born into a middle-class Jewish family. I had no real idea who Jesus was. I actually believed Jesus's last name was Christ, that He was the son of Mr. and Mrs. Christ! My ambition was to earn an advanced degree in business, become a multimillionaire by age thirty, and live a comfortable life. I believed in God, but He did not really figure into my plans for my life.

I would have laughed if someone had told me then that I would become a Messianic rabbi, a "clergyman." I would have known they were crazy if they had said I'd become president and CEO of Jewish Voice Ministries International—an organization devoted to reaching Jewish people around the world with the message of eternal life through faith in the Messiah, Jesus of Nazareth.

But that was God's plan for me—and He aligned all the steps necessary to bring it about in His time. I won't go into detail about all that right now. You can read about it in my book *A Rabbi Looks at Jesus of Nazareth.*

But the point I want to make is that God had a specific plan in mind for me, and He has one for you as well. Although He gave me clear direction, it was up to me to find that plan and follow it. I could have rebelled against it, but I didn't—and I am so glad!

God's plan for you will make you glad, too!

YOU ARE AMONG THE ELECT

As you read through the New Testament scriptures, you will find numerous references to "the elect." God elected (or chose) *you* to be a part of His family. This is not a group choosing, like His selection of the nation of Israel to be His people, but rather God's call to you individually to adopt you as His child.

All things are under God's control—and He will reveal and fulfill His plan to those who belong to Him and seek to do His will. You can be sure that if you are sold out to God and seeking His kingdom above all else (Matt. 6:33), His plan for you will line up with the desires of your heart.

A QUICK HEBREW LESSON

I want to give you a little Hebrew lesson to help you understand one of God's most precious promises—not just to the Jewish people, but to you. Most of you were required to take a foreign language when you were in high school, but I'm sure that very few of you chose to study Hebrew. Even so, you probably know more Hebrew words than you realize.

For example, have you ever said, "Hallelujah"? That's a Hebrew word that we use today. It is a compound of the Hebrew word *halal*, which means praise, and what we call the tetragrammaton, the name of God—YHVH (יהוה), often pronounced as "Yaweh" or "Jehovah," although Jews do not pronounce this name. Instead, we say "Adonai" or "HaShem."

When we say "Hallelujah," we are recognizing God's sovereign nature. He is the only one who is worthy of our praise and worship. Linguists say this word is never translated as it passes from language to language. Think, for example, about the word *Spanish*. If you were to actually say that word in Spanish, it would be *Español*. If you were to say *United States* in Spanish, it would be translated as *Estados Unidos*. But hallelujah never changes. Instead, people of many different cultures and faiths say "hallelujah" to praise the name of the Lord.

Another Hebrew word we all use today is *amen*. It carries the idea of agreement with what has been said. The literal meaning is "let it be so" or "let it come to pass."

So the good news is that you're starting out with at least a couple of Hebrew words. As we look at the passage from Jeremiah 29, I will share several more that you can add to your Hebrew vocabulary. I often tell people in the seminars and conferences where I speak that when they repeat Hebrew words I teach them, it makes me feel at home.

What God's Plan Doesn't Involve

Before we move on to a discussion of what God's plan for you *is*, let's talk for just a moment about what it *is not*. God's plan does not involve:

- The pursuit of riches, which the Bible calls "chasing after the wind" (Eccles. 2:11).

- The pursuit of fame. Jesus had harsh words for those who were anxious to be recognized and esteemed by others (Matt. 6:5).

- The pursuit of personal comfort and an easy, care-free life of indifference. Jesus told us to be ready to take up our cross daily and follow Him (Luke 9:23).

Does this mean it's wrong to be rich, famous, or comfortable? Not at all. God's ultimate plan might be for you to be any or all of these things. But if so, they will result from you doing whatever it is that God wants you to do—not from anything you do to bring them about.

God's plan is far better than any of these things. It brings eternal blessings, peace, and well-being far beyond anything as fleeting as worldly wealth, fame, or pleasure.

I believe that God wants you to be safe, secure, and healthy in body, mind, and spirit. He wants you to take care of yourself, because that's the only way you'll have the strength and ability to bless others. And the Bible promises in Romans 8:28–30:

> Now we know that all things work together for good for those who love God, who are called according to His purpose. For those whom He foreknew He also predestined to be conformed to the image of His Son, so that He might be the firstborn among many brothers and sisters. And those whom He predestined, He also called; and those whom He called, He also justified; and those whom He justified, He also glorified.

By the way, I think it is perfectly fine for Christians to want good things for themselves. God doesn't expect us to be doormats who let other people walk all over us and never ask for a thing for ourselves.

Jesus said that we are to love our neighbors as much as we love ourselves. This implies that it's OK to love yourself. God understands that self-love is a powerful force, and He appeals to it to teach us how we are supposed to love others. He wants us to love other people so much that we hurt with them when they are sick, hungry, cold, poor, lost, or suffering in other ways.

The Apostle Paul put it this way:

> For no one ever hated his own flesh, but nourishes and cherishes it—just as Messiah also does His community, because we are members of His body.
> —Ephesians 5:29–30

Even Jesus, our Messiah, the most giving and unselfish person ever to walk this planet, had needs. He took steps to meet them, and often let others have the privilege of ministering to Him. For example:

- He accepted the hospitality offered by Mary, Martha, and their brother Lazarus (Luke 10:38–42).

- He was often a dinner guest in other people's homes (Luke 7:36; 14:1; 19:5).

- When He was weary from long days of teaching and healing, He withdrew to a private place to rest (Mark 6:30–31).

- He did not object when Mary anointed Him with an extremely expensive bottle of perfume (Luke 7:36–50; John 11:2).

Maybe you don't see yourself the same way God does. You might be smiling to yourself and thinking, "Me? Do something important for God? No way!" If that's how you feel, you're in very good company:

- When God called Moses to lead the children of Israel out of Egypt, Moses replied, "Lord, I have never been eloquent, neither in the past nor since you have spoken to your servant. I am slow of speech and tongue...Please send someone else" (Exod. 4:10, 13, NIV).

- When Gideon was chosen to rescue Israel from the Midianites, he said, "But how can I save Israel? My clan is the weakest in Manasseh, and I am the least in my family" (Judg. 6:15, NIV).

- When the time came for Samuel to anoint Saul as the first king of Israel, he couldn't find him because Saul was hiding. Saul also took a page from Gideon's book, protesting that he didn't deserve to be king. "But am I not a Benjamite, from the smallest tribe in Israel, and is not my clan the least of all the clans of the tribe of Benjamin?" (1 Sam. 9:21, NIV). Sadly for Saul, his humility did not last.

The Bible is full of similar examples:

- David was the youngest and least impressive in his family when God chose him to replace Saul as king (1 Sam. 16:11–13).

- And when the prophet Isaiah saw a vision of the Lord, he said, "Woe to me! I am ruined! For I am a man of unclean lips" (Isa. 6:5, NIV).

None of these men thought they could do anything for God. But He knew better. In fact, He knew them better than they knew themselves—just as He knows you better than you know yourself. David got it right when he wrote:

> Whenever I sit down or stand up, You know it. You discern my thinking from afar. You observe my journeying and my resting and You are familiar with all my ways. Even before a word is on my tongue, behold, Adonai, You know all about it.
>
> —Psalm 139:2–4

Again, God knows you better than anyone else knows you. And if He believes you can do great things, who are you to disagree?

You Are Unique

I understand that it's easy to feel insignificant in a world that contains more than seven billion people. Everyone knows that one billion people is a huge number. How can we put this into proper perspective? Consider these facts from *How Much Is a Million?* by David M. Schwartz.

How much is a billion? "If you sat down to count from one to one billion, you would be counting for ninety-five years."[1]

Now, multiply a billion by seven, and you begin to have some idea of just how many men, women, and children there are in the world.

Logically it makes sense to think that if you closely examined the personal traits of everyone on earth, you would find a few perfect matches. It would seem that with a number that big, there's just bound to be some overlap. But there isn't. Every human being is a unique creature, designed by a creative and loving God.

- No other human being has your DNA.

- Nobody else has your unique fingerprints.

- No other person has your unique voice pattern.

- No one else has had the experiences you've had, has thought your thoughts, or learned exactly what you learned through your years in school.

- Even identical twins are not really identical at all.

Despite the huge number of people on this planet, God is deeply concerned about the needs of every single human being. Because He is God, He is able to deal with you as if you were the only person on earth. Yeshua died so that sinners could be pardoned and reconciled with God. Never forget that if you had been the *only* sinner, He would have given His life for you alone. Such is the width and depth of God's love and wisdom.

Jesus taught that God even knows how many hairs you have on your head (Matt. 10:30). If you have an "average" head of hair, that means you have somewhere between 110,000 and 150,000 individual hairs, depending on your hair color. (Blondes tend to have more individual hairs than others; redheads the least.)[2]

God knows how many hairs you have because He fashioned every follicle Himself. He is like the new father and mother who count their little one's fingers and toes over and over again because their hearts are so full of love for their child. God doesn't know all these things because He is into trivia, but because He loves you enough to keep track of the number of hairs on your head. So you can be sure He loves you enough to develop a unique plan for your life.

God's plan and purpose for your life is a unique calling and destiny that only you and you alone can fulfill. Just as your fingerprints and DNA are unique to you and you alone, so is your divine destiny. No one else alive or who has ever lived has the same exact destiny God has ordained for you.

Your Impact Is Greater
Than You Know

Let me tell you something else. If you belong to God and are living for Him, God knows that you have within you the power and ability to change the world.

The eighteenth chapter of Genesis contains an account of a conversation between Abraham and God, after God decided to destroy Sodom because of its wickedness. Abraham wanted to save the life of his nephew Lot, who lived in Sodom, so he asked, "What if there are fifty righteous people in the city? Will you spare the entire city for the sake of fifty?"

"Yes," God said, "I will spare the city for the sake of fifty."

"What about forty-five?" Abraham asked. "Will you spare Sodom for forty-five righteous people?"

Abraham kept lowering the number until God finally agreed to spare the city if ten righteous people could be found there. Tragically for Sodom, it didn't happen, and the place was annihilated. (See Genesis 18:16–33.)

But the point is that a few righteous people could have saved it. A spark of goodness would have prevented destruction.

Who can say what enormous impact your godly behavior will have on your community? When the people of Nineveh repented after Jonah preached to them, their city was spared. It is a biblical principle that righteous, obedient people bring life and peace to their cities.

A Good Promise in a Bad Chapter

Now I want to share something that makes Jeremiah 29:11 even more interesting: it comes in the middle of a bad chapter.

What do I mean by that? This wonderful promise from the Lord of good plans of hope and a future came in the midst of one of the worst times in Israel's history! Jeremiah, otherwise known as "the weeping prophet," was writing these words to Jews who had been carried away into exile from the southern kingdom of Judah, destroyed in 586 BC. They were now living in Babylon as prisoners of the powerful King Nebuchadnezzar. They were separated from their families, unable to worship freely, toiling as slaves in a foreign land.

Whatever you are facing today, the situation facing the Jews of the sixth century BC was much, much worse. But even then, despite their history of rebellion and disobedience, God remained faithful. His plan and desire was and always has been to prosper His chosen people Israel and give them hope and a future. This same plan is true for all of us; and it is true for *you*.

Chapter 2

WHAT HOLDS YOU CAPTIVE?

The Spirit of the Lord is on me, because he has anointed me to proclaim good news to the poor. He has sent me to proclaim freedom for the prisoners and recovery of sight for the blind, to set the oppressed free, to proclaim the year of the Lord's favor.

—LUKE 4:18–19, NIV

I T IS A rare person who isn't held captive by something. You may be a prisoner of:

- Sin

- Fear

- Loneliness

- Rejection

- Insecurity

- Debilitating illness

- Sex

- Alcohol or drug addiction

- Poverty

- Or a very long list of other things. You fill in the blanks.

But in the midst of whatever captivity we face, there is always the promise of freedom, of liberty, of victory. In the midst of the darkest oppression, we can cling to the promise of Yeshua, who says: "So if the Son sets you free, you will be free indeed" (John 8:36, NIV)!

THE FUTURE SEEMED LOST

As I mentioned in the previous chapter, when God declared through Jeremiah, "For I know the plans that I have in mind for you," He was speaking to the Jews living in captivity in the country of Babylonia.

What we refer to as "the Babylonian captivity" actually took place in stages. In the first invasion of Jerusalem, Daniel and a large population of young Jews were taken to Babylon, and the temple built by Solomon was demolished. Later, the entire city of Jerusalem was destroyed, and thousands of Jews were either slaughtered or taken captive.

As I already mentioned, this was a terrible time for the Jewish people, one of the worst times in our history (along with slavery in Egypt and the earlier Assyrian invasion of the northern tribes of Israel). It seemed all hope was lost. Psalm 137:1–6 paints a picture of what it was like for them living as slaves in exile:

> By the rivers of Babylon, we sat down and wept, when we remembered Zion. On the willows there we hung up our harps. For there our captors demanded songs and our tormentors asked for joy: "Sing us one of the songs of Zion." How can we sing a song of ADONAI in a foreign land? If I forget you, O Jerusalem, let my right hand wither. May my tongue cling to the roof of my mouth if I cease to remember you, if I do not set Jerusalem above my chief joy.

The children of Israel who received the promise of God through Jeremiah were in terrible shape. They were prisoners of an ungodly foreign government. They were cut off from their worship, and their temple had been desecrated. They were separated from their homes and their families. They were cut off from their entire way of life, and naturally, they were longing to return to their homeland of Israel.

It's difficult to imagine the despair and hopelessness the Jewish people must have felt during this period of exile and captivity. It wasn't that life was always horrible for them. By most accounts, the Jews that were carried into Babylon were not treated cruelly during the entirety of their captivity. Over time, they were allowed to become merchants, teachers, and even government officials. They were also allowed to preserve their culture, building a strong Jewish community that thrived until just a few decades ago.

What Nebuchadnezzar did was empty the Land of Promise of its artists and intellectuals. He took the writers, poets, mathematicians, engineers, and teachers and left behind a poor society consisting largely of subsistence farmers.

The most tragic thing he did was destroy the magnificent temple and leave the city of Jerusalem in ruins. The city of splendor where David and Solomon had reigned stood desolate for over one hundred years. Its gates were thrown down, and many of its beautiful buildings burned to the ground. All the great treasures had been looted from the temple and carried back to Babylon.

The identity and religious life of the Jewish people were deeply connected to the city of Jerusalem and the temple. The Jews, as God's chosen people, were to be a kingdom of priests, a holy nation, a light to the heathen nations that surrounded them. God had promised throughout the Torah and prophets that a Messiah would come through them and bless all families of the earth. (See Genesis 12:1–3.) This promised Messiah would restore Israel to its former glory under King David and transform the world back to a pre-Adamic paradise, *Gan-Aden* (גן עדן), a garden of Eden. But in captivity, all of these things seemed to vanish. They were now just empty promises. After years of captivity, most had lost hope. They were no longer able to see God at work in their lives, and they didn't believe He cared about them. They were at rock bottom. But through all of their suffering and despair, God *was* with them. In fact, He revealed Himself (and I believe His promised Redeemer, the Messiah) at perhaps the lowest point of their captivity.

Their worst moment came when King Nebuchadnezzar set up a huge idol made of gold and demanded that everyone in Babylon—including Jews—bow down and worship it. Anyone who refused to obey the king's order was to be executed.

The Jews were caught in a terrible dilemma. They had to choose between obedience to God and obedience to the king of Babylon. Perhaps some of their Babylonian neighbors said to them, "Oh, come on, it's not going to hurt you to worship the idol just this once. We all know your heart's not in it. Just do it to please the king. After all, there are many paths to God."

Have you ever heard anything like that? I have. But I've also learned that it's not true. There is one path to God, and that is through faith in the Messiah, Yeshua, who says, "I am the way and the truth and the life. No one comes to the Father except through me" (John 14:6, NIV).

Some Jews might have been tempted to think, "Maybe it can't hurt to bow down to the golden idol. After all, we've spent our entire lives worshipping the God of Abraham, Isaac, and Jacob, and look what it got us—captivity in a foreign land." But if they were honest with themselves, they couldn't say they had been faithful to God's commandments because it was their worship of idols that caused God to deliver them into the hands of their oppressors. Undoubtedly, some Jews did bow down to the idol. But most wouldn't. King Nebuchadnezzar was livid and decided to make an example of three young men—Shadrach, Meshach, and Abednego. They were bound hand and foot and thrown into a superheated furnace. The king was so outraged that he ordered the furnace to be heated seven times hotter than usual. The flames were so hot, in fact, that when the furnace was opened so the three victims could be thrown into the fire, flames leapt out and killed the soldiers who were holding them.

But Shadrach, Meshach, and Abednego were not harmed. Instead, the king looked into the furnace and saw four men walking around in there. Nebuchadnezzar asked his attendants, "Weren't there three men that we tied up and threw into the fire? Look! I see four men walking around in the fire, unbound and unharmed, and the fourth looks like a son of the gods."

The Bible says:

> Nebuchadnezzar then approached the opening of the blazing furnace and shouted, "Shadrach, Meshach and Abednego, servants of the Most High God, come out! Come here!"
>
> So Shadrach, Meshach and Abednego came out of the fire, and the satraps, prefects, governors and royal advisers crowded around them. They saw that the fire had not harmed their bodies, nor was a hair of their heads singed; their robes were not scorched, and there was no smell of fire on them.
>
> Then Nebuchadnezzar said, "Praise be to the God of Shadrach, Meshach and Abednego, who has sent his angel and rescued his servants! They trusted in him and defied the king's command and were willing to give up their lives rather than serve or worship any god except their own God. Therefore I decree that the people of any nation or language who say anything against the God of Shadrach, Meshach and Abednego be cut into pieces and their houses be turned into piles of rubble, for no other god can save in this way."
>
> —Daniel 3:26–29, niv

In the moment of greatest trial and challenge, God showed up. I believe it was Yeshua, in His preincarnate form, with them in that furnace. It was only because they were thrown into the fire that these three young heroes encountered the Son of God. The same thing happens to us when we find ourselves in the fire. We may not escape the flames entirely, but God will meet us there, and He promises to always be with us:

> When you pass through the waters, I will be with you; and when you pass through the rivers, they will not sweep over you. When you walk through the fire, you will not be burned; the flames will not set you ablaze. For I am the LORD your God, the Holy One of Israel, your Savior.
> —ISAIAH 43:2–3, NIV

BAD TIMES

As we can see from the story of the fiery furnace, God was still with the Jewish people in their time of trouble. Even so, it was a very difficult period in their history.

To be totally honest about it, the whole Book of Jeremiah is "a bad book." It's heartbreaking. Because of their disobedience, the children of Israel had been led off into captivity. Yet it's in the midst of this bad chapter, in the middle of a bad book, that we find God's wonderful promise of hope and a future for His people.

And, by the way, God makes many other promises in the Book of Jeremiah—promises to preserve the Jewish people, promises to bring them back to their land, promises to restore them spiritually, and promises that He will provide a New Covenant, where He will remove their sin and remember it no more. He also makes repeated declarations of His faithfulness and unceasing love.

One such scripture is Jeremiah 31:3, where God declares, "I have loved you with an everlasting love" (NIV). What a wonderful promise to cling to when things aren't going quite the way we want them to.

Perhaps you are reading this in the midst of a bad chapter in your life. It could be that you're going through family difficulties or facing challenges with your health, finances, or career. Most of us rarely have a time when we're not experiencing some sort of trial. Maybe you feel that God has abandoned you because He did not do something you had hoped He would, or He allowed you to go through something you expected He would resolve.

But I have good news for you. In the midst of whatever trial or tribulation you may be going through right now—or that may come your way tomorrow—the Lord has a wonderful promise for you. Jeremiah 29:11 is not only a good verse in the midst of a "bad" chapter but also a good verse in the midst of a "bad" book!

Maybe you're not just going through a bad chapter in your life. Perhaps your whole life has been plagued by sorrows, and you don't understand why you should be singled out for such pain. When people tell you, "God knows how much you can handle," or, "God must think an awful lot of you to trust you with such burdens," it's almost more than you can bear.

But what you may not realize is that everyone you know is dealing with some type of issue. Although it may appear different, in reality no one sails through this life on calm seas and under sunny skies. In many meetings I've spoken at over the years, I've asked people who were suffering from severe depression or discouragement to come forward for prayer. Many times, half of the audience has responded: men, women, teenagers, and children of all ages. From just looking at them, you couldn't tell that anything was wrong. But plenty was wrong.

Looks are deceiving. Many *are* suffering, and you may be one of them.

You and I run into people every day who are suffering inside, and we know nothing about it. It might be the person behind the counter at the dry cleaners. The waitress in the café. The fellow behind the window at the DMV. Trouble is everywhere. But God is everywhere, too. And there is no problem so big or bad that He can't handle it and turn it to your advantage!

Consider what happened one cold March night about fifty years ago at West Side Baptist Church in Beatrice, Nebraska. The story may sound like an urban legend—something a gullible friend might forward to you via e-mail—but it's absolutely true.[1]

It was 7:25 p.m., and even though choir practice was scheduled to begin at 7:20, the church sanctuary was empty. Pastor Walter Klempel was at home, waiting for his teenage daughter to get ready. Another teen, Ladonna Vandergrift, was struggling with a geometry problem and had lost track of the time. Sisters Royena and Sadie Estes couldn't get their car started. Herbert Kipf was trying to finish writing a letter he'd been putting off. And so on. Every member of the choir had some difficulty that kept him or her from getting to the church on time.

At precisely 7:25, just as they should have been halfway through their first song, a thunderous explosion ripped through the building. Later that night, as investigators sifted through the rubble, they determined that the explosion was the result of a gas leak in the furnace—located just below the choir loft. Had the choir members been in that loft, every one of them would have been killed.

Yes, God is more than capable of working everything together for our good—even those events that seem annoying and frustrating when taken by themselves. The big picture is always in God's hands.

In his book *Run With the Horses* Eugene H. Peterson writes about Israel's exile in Babylon and how that experience relates to us today.

> Israel's exile was a violent and extreme form of what all of us experience from time to time. Inner experiences of exile take place even if we never move from the street on which we were brought up. We are exiled from the womb and begin life in strange and harsh surroundings. We are exiled from our homes at an early age and find ourselves in the terrifying and demanding world of school. We are exiled from school and have to make our way the best we can in the world of work. We are exiled from our hometowns and have to find our way in new states and cities.
>
> These experiences of exile, minor and major, continue through changes in society, changes in government, changes in values, changes in our bodies, our emotions, our families and marriages. We barely get used to one set of circumstances and faces when we are forced to deal with another. The exile experienced by the Hebrews is a dramatic instance of what we all experience simply by being alive in this world. Repeatedly we find ourselves in circumstances where we are not at home. We are "strangers in a strange land."
>
> The essential meaning of exile is that we are where we don't want to be. We are separated from home...We are forced to be away from the place where we comprehend and appreciate our surroundings. We are forced to be away from that which is most congenial to us. It is an experience of dislocation—everything is out of joint. Nothing fits together.[2]

Even when we feel as if we are living in exile, God wants us to trust Him, to press forward and "fight the good fight of faith" (1 Tim. 6:12, MEV). The last thing He wants us to do is sit around feeling sorry for ourselves, waiting passively for things to change. Fretting and feeling sorry for ourselves accomplishes absolutely nothing; it is a waste of time. Always remember that God wants to bless you even in the midst of the trials of life.

Peterson writes that Israel's time in exile "became the most creative period in the entire sweep of Hebrew history. They did not lose their identity; they discovered it. They learned how to pray in deeper and more life-changing ways than ever. They wrote and copied and pondered the vast revelation that had come down to them from Moses and the prophets, and they came to recognize the incredible riches of their Scriptures. They found that God was not dependent on a place; he was not tied to familiar surroundings. The violent dislocation of the exile shook them out of their comfortable but reality-distorting assumptions and allowed them to see depths and heights that they had never even imagined before. They lost everything that they thought was important and found what was important: they found God."[3] In fact, the greatest body of literature ever produced in Judaism, the Babylonian Talmud, was compiled over centuries of exile in Babylon.

I know some people who are completely focused on end-time prophecy and when Jesus will return. They expect it to happen any day now—and I'm not about to argue with them. I believe the signs of His coming are all around us. I also admire these people because they are living in obedience to our Lord's command:

> Therefore stay alert; for you do not know what day your
> Lord is coming.
>
> —MATTHEW 24:42

But at the same time, I'm afraid that some of these well-meaning, faithful folks aren't investing their time and energy in the work God wants us to be doing while there is still opportunity. Instead, they're just waiting. Like Yeshua, we must work while it is yet day for night will come when no man can work (see John 9:4). While we are still on this earth, we are to be coworkers with the Lord to expand His kingdom and bring in the harvest.

THE CAREFREE LIFE?

At some point in life, we all experience the pain of feeling like we are living in exile. One reason I think this happens is because many Christians have a misconception that when we accept Jesus, all of our problems are going to disappear, and life from then on will be just tiptoeing through the tulips. But there's nothing in the Bible that promises you a carefree life. On the contrary, Yeshua said, "If they persecuted Me, they will also persecute you" (John 15:20, MEV). Just as He was rejected and reviled, you also will experience the same when you stand up for your beliefs. Don't be surprised or dejected when this happens. Expect it, and rejoice when it does.

The promise that we receive when we walk with the Lord is not that we will be removed from adversity. Rather, the promise is, "He who is in you is greater than he who is in the world" (1 John 4:4, MEV), and that we can be "more than conquerors through Him who loved us" (Rom. 8:37, MEV). Do you see that?

There's a big difference between those two approaches and assumptions about life.

I want to encourage you with these words. If you've gone through a terrible trial, a horrible tribulation, and you just haven't found the victory, then I want to turn your attention to one of the greatest promises in Scripture. This promise says that God sees your needs and He cares about you.

Look at how Jeremiah 29:11–14 begins. It says, "'For I know the plans I have for you,' declares the LORD, 'plans to prosper you...'" (NIV). Let me focus your attention on the pronoun that appears twice at the beginning: *you*. It's easy to look at the people around you and believe that God has a plan for them. "Oh, my goodness, look at how God is using him (or her)." "Listen to the way he preaches." "Look at that woman of faith!" "Look at what God has done through him." "He's a great man of God, but what do I have to offer? "God cares about him, but would He care about me?"

It's easy to believe that God cares about us as a corporate body—that He cares about His people. The challenge is believing that He cares about us as individuals—that He cares about you and me. But He does. In fact, Jesus said that God knows every time a sparrow falls to the ground (Matt. 10:29). Over the years, I have prayed for thousands of people, and I can exercise faith to believe with somebody else that God will drive the cancer from their body, or heal their damaged back, or deliver them from some disease, restore their family, or provide for their need. But when it comes to believing God for my own health, my own healing, my own deliverance, my own family, or my own needs, that's a far greater challenge.

I've been praying for the salvation of my Jewish mother and sister for more than thirty years! Are they saved? Net yet. But

I am still confident they will be. I'm claiming the promise that salvation is not only for me but for my entire household, according to Acts 16:31.

It's a challenge for me to share my faith with my mother and with the members of my immediate family. It's easier for others to talk to them, whereas it's easier for me to share the gospel with people I don't know very well. When it comes to believing God for "me," that's a real challenge compared to believing for "we."

But this passage from Jeremiah by application is not only for the Jewish people, nor is it only for God's people corporately. He has a plan for you individually. That plan for your life was established before you were ever created. And He is committed to fulfilling that plan in and through you, regardless of how you feel or the circumstances you are currently facing.

FAITH AND OBEDIENCE ARE THE KEYS

Faith in God—believing that "He exists and that He is a rewarder of those who diligently seek Him" (Heb. 11:6, MEV)—and obedience to His will are the keys to unlocking His plan for your life. And the first act of obedience is surrendering control of your life to the Lord, acknowledging Jesus as Messiah and Savior and inviting Him into your life.

Perhaps you've already done this. But even if you've already given your heart and life to Him, please take a few moments right now to rededicate yourself to living daily in faith and obedience. Although accepting the gift of salvation is a one-time thing, surrender to the Lord is a decision we must make on a daily basis. Not a day goes by that we are not tempted to follow our own selfish wills instead of His. Jesus put it this way: "If anyone wants to follow after Me, he must deny himself, take up his cross, and follow Me" (Matt. 16:24).

If you have not yet accepted Him into your life, why not do it right now? He loves you and wants to change your life forever. He wants to forgive you and restore you. All you have to do is invite Him into your life. When you do, real life begins.

GOD DESIRES TO BLESS YOU

Psalm 37:4 (NIV) says, "Take delight in the LORD, and he will give you the desires of your heart." What are the desires of *your* heart? Are they in line with the will of God? Clearly, some desires are godly and others aren't—and ungodly desires are almost always a perversion of godly ones.

There are so many things that are good and holy in and of themselves, but if they are mishandled they become extremely dangerous. Think about water. No human being can survive for long without water. And yet the International Life Saving Federation says as many as 1.2 million people drown every year around the world. That's more than two people every minute.[4]

Nuclear power is another example. Used properly, it could meet the world's energy needs. Used improperly, it could destroy the world. It seems that every good gift or desire God gives to sustain and enhance life can be perverted and turned into something destructive. This is just one important reason why it's so important to follow God's will in everything we do.

What does God want you to do? If you like sports, think of it this way. Suppose your favorite football team signed nine kickers. No quarterbacks. No receivers. No linemen. Just kickers. You'd think the general manager had lost his mind, and you'd be in for a very long season.

God gave us all different talents and abilities because we all have unique paths to follow and unique purposes to fulfill. He expects us to work together in harmony to carry out His purposes.

In 1 Corinthians 12:14–18 Paul writes:

> For the body is not one part, but many. If the foot says, "Since I'm not a hand, I'm not part of the body," is it therefore not part of the body? And if the ear says, "Since I'm not an eye, I'm not part of the body," is it for this reason any less part of the body? If the whole body were an eye, where would the hearing be? If the whole were hearing, where would the sense of smell be? But now God has placed the parts—each one of them—in the body just as He desired.

Some people have very healthy self-esteem. Others suffer from feelings of inadequacy and inferiority. Yet every person has important talents and abilities that were given by God. Some, because of the nature of their gifts, may be in the spotlight. Others stay in the background. But the person who gets recognition is no more important than the person who works quietly behind the scenes. God sees things much differently than we do, and He's never dazzled by talent or celebrity.

It is vitally important that you learn to use the abilities God has given you. Don't try to be something you're not. Don't offer to sing a solo during the worship service if you're tone deaf. But please don't hide your talent and let false modesty or low self-esteem prevent you from accomplishing great things for God.

Here are four important means God uses to reveal His plans for us:

1. The Bible

This does not mean that you can open the Bible at random, point to a verse, and read, "I want you to go into medicine." It doesn't work that way. Perhaps you've heard about the young man who tried to use that method to find God's will. The first verse he turned to said, "Judas went out and hanged himself." He quickly turned to another section, jabbed his finger at the book, and this time he read, "Go thou and do likewise."

Obviously that's not the way to use the Bible. The Bible will help you by revealing God's will in a general sense. As we mentioned earlier, there are certain things no believer can do because they are simply contrary to God's laws. Could a believer deal drugs? Could he feel at ease working as a black-jack dealer in Las Vegas? Could a follower of Jesus own and operate sweatshops overseas?

Every individual Bible believer must make up his or her mind about these and dozens of similar issues. The best way to know for sure what is right or wrong for you is to study the Bible. If you have a hard time squaring your life plans with God's Word, it's probably time to rethink the path you're on.

2. Prayer

Prayer is a two-way street. It involves not only talking to God but listening to Him as well—and that means spending time sitting before Him in silence, waiting to hear His voice. Ask Him for direction, and He will provide it. You may receive an impression, or a particular scripture. Or you may find that your prayer is answered through what your friends say to you during the day that follows. The important thing is to know that God is concerned about you and will respond if you ask Him to.

James, the brother of Jesus, wrote:

> But if any of you lacks wisdom, let him ask of God, who gives to all without hesitation and without reproach; and it will be given to him.
>
> —JAMES 1:5

Prayer works!

3. Wise counsel of others

Proverbs 19:20 says, "Listen to advice and accept instruction, so that in the end you may be wise." This doesn't mean we're supposed to follow every bit of advice that comes our way. We should test everything against the Word of God for confirmation. Much of the well-meaning advice our friends give us is worthless. Far too often our "friends" only tell us what they think we want to hear. But we all need to have people in our lives who are willing to tell us the truth whether or not we want to hear it.

The Bible tells of many kings who failed because they only listened to prophets who stroked their egos and promised them victory. In other words, they surrounded themselves with "yes-men" who told them to do what they wanted to do in the first place. And that sort of behavior always leads to tragedy. We can't cherry-pick the advice we want to hear but must look for the overall consensus of people we trust and respect.

Another great verse from Proverbs says, "For lack of guidance a nation falls, but victory is won through many advisers" (Prov. 11:14, NIV).

4. Circumstances

Do you suppose it was just luck that Peter and John happened to be washing their nets on the side of the Sea of Galilee the day Jesus called them to be His disciples? (See Luke 5:1–11.) Did the Samaritan woman just happen to be going to the well the morning Jesus asked her for a drink? (See John 4:1–42.) Or had it all been seen beforehand?

Many times God speaks through the circumstances that come into our lives. But we'll never know it if we don't keep our eyes and ears open.

Here's an important point to remember: *Never rely on circumstances alone.* Your present situation is merely one of the indicators that can show whether you're moving in the right direction. You shouldn't let circumstances alone hold you back from moving forward if every other indicator says, "Go!" Nor should you decide to move forward, based on circumstances alone, if every other indicator says, "Stop!"

If everything else lines up—the desires of your heart, your talents and abilities, counsel from people you trust, God's Word, and prayer—then look for circumstances to line up as well, and for God to open up a way for you to move ahead in the path He's chosen for you.

GOD WANTS TO SPEND TIME WITH YOU

If you want to know God's plan for your life, it makes sense that you will spend time with Him, seeking His guidance, protection, and blessing. Some people are so busy that they let God become an afterthought. They may mumble a few words of prayer as they fall into bed at night, or say grace over breakfast, but that's about it, except for services on the weekend.

Having a solid relationship with God is an extremely important part of a satisfied, fulfilling life. God wants His people to talk to Him, listen for His voice, meditate on His Word, and seek His guidance and counsel.

There is nothing more beneficial to the development of human character than spending time with God. It is in His presence that we truly come to understand who He is—and who we are. It is here that we can be transformed into His likeness. As author George MacDonald said, "The purposes of God point to one simple end—that we should be as He is, think the same thoughts, mean the same things, possess the same blessedness."[5]

Anyone who really wants to know God's plans for their life should spend time with Him every day.

Chapter 3

WHY DO WE STRUGGLE TO BELIEVE GOD'S PROMISES?

The LORD is trustworthy in all he promises and faithful in all he does.

—PSALM 145:13, NIV

WHY IS IT so hard for us to believe that God has a plan for our individual lives? I can think of several reasons. Allow me to expand on the top three.

Sometimes We Feel Forgotten

You may ask, "If God loves me, then why did He allow me to go through this terrible circumstance?" Or, "If God loves me, why did He cause this to happen to me?"

As a result of the things that we experience, we become distrustful and our faith falters. Also, although we may not realize it, we hold God accountable for something we don't think He should have allowed to happen to us. In effect, we start carrying a grudge against God.

There have been many times in my own life when I haven't understood what God was doing. It was only later on, when I looked back on the situation, that I saw His purposes clearly. I was looking at things from my limited human perspective. God was looking at everything from an eternal perspective. As human beings, we are limited by space and time, and we must live our lives in one direction, from start to finish.

But God is above space and time, and sees everything from every conceivable angle at once. You might think of it like shooting a movie. As you probably know, when a director films a movie, he does not shoot it in chronological order. Instead, all or most of the scenes that take place in a certain location are filmed first. In some cases, the ending may be filmed first and the beginning last. Then the whole thing is edited together so it makes perfect sense. Similarly, when God sees your life—or mine—it's like He's picking up a length of film, holding it up to the light, and seeing the whole thing at once.

He knows where some improvements are needed—where you have to be a little stronger, bolder, or more courageous. He sees the places where you're in danger of falling. I'm not saying your life is like a movie or a game. It is much more serious than that, and the consequences are eternal. But it will help us have a proper understanding if we pray for God to give us His perspective on things.

As I said, there are so many times I look back on my life and think, "Oh, I get it now!" There may be times when we feel God is giving us more than we can bear, but His Word says He will never do that. First Corinthians 10:13 tells us, "No temptation has taken hold of you except what is common to mankind. But God is faithful—He will not allow you to be tempted beyond what you can handle. But with the temptation He will also provide a way of escape, so you will be able to endure it." It may feel like more than you can bear, but only God knows how much you truly can handle, and He will never take you beyond that point.

Maybe you feel forgotten today. If so, I want to remind you that God *does* see you. He *does* have a plan for you. He loves you and He *does* care intimately for you. He is always faithful and has not forgotten you, no matter how forgotten you may feel!

SOMETIMES WE FEEL INSIGNIFICANT

You may ask, "Who am I? What do I have to offer?" You may think, "I can't sing and I can't preach. I can't play an instrument. What do I have to offer?"

Jeremiah felt the same way. The prophet responded to God's call by saying:

"Alas, Sovereign Lord...I do not know how to speak; I am too young."

But the Lord said to me, "Do not say, 'I am too young.' You must go to everyone I send you to and say whatever I command you. Do not be afraid of them, for I am with you and will rescue you," declares the Lord.

Then the Lord reached out his hand and touched my mouth and said to me, "I have put my words in your mouth. See, today I appoint you over nations and kingdoms to uproot and tear down, to destroy and overthrow, to build and to plant."

—Jeremiah 1:6–10, niv

God had to remind him, "Before I formed you in the womb, I knew you" (Jer. 1:5). When God called him, Jeremiah downplayed his abilities. God told him, "Don't say you're a child or that you're insignificant. I have called you to go to the nations. I have anointed you. I have a destiny for your life."

On the authority of God's Word, I tell you that He has a destiny, a plan, and a purpose for *your* life. He has deposited gifts and talents within you that you may not even be aware of. He has ordained a destiny for your life that is different from that of anyone else in the entire world. It's a trap to say things like, "I'm insignificant," or, "I have nothing to offer." Remember the parable of the talents (Matt. 25:14–30). The first two who used their talents and abilities for the master were rewarded. But the one who buried his talent because of fear and did nothing was punished. Do not bury your God-given gifts and talents in the sand. Use them for His glory. You have significance in God. You have a purpose!

SOMETIMES WE FEEL CONDEMNED

"How could God forgive me for that terrible thing I did? After all, I should be a mature believer. I know better. I let my family down. I let God down, and He won't forgive me." Thoughts like these cause us to walk in guilt and condemnation. On the outside, we may still smile and raise our hands and do all the things we know to do. But inside, we're weighed down with condemnation and guilt.

Let's take a quick look at some heroes from the Bible, and see how they stack up:

HEROES IN THE BIBLE	
Noah	Drunkenness
Abraham	Lied about Sarah's identity
Jacob	Swindled his father and brother
Moses	Murdered an Egyptian
David	Committed adultery and murder
Gideon	Idolatry
Solomon	Idolatry
Peter	Denied Jesus three times

One of the many things I appreciate about the Bible is that it tells it like it is. There's no whitewashing; there are no perfect individuals. We get to see everybody, warts and all.

Take Peter, the last name on our list. How do you think he felt after denying three times that he knew Jesus? What must have made it even worse for Peter was that he turned away from Jesus at the exact moment when his Master needed him the most.

And remember, when Jesus told Peter that he would deny Him, the apostle declared, "Master, I am ready to go with You even to prison and to death!" (Luke 22:33). No wonder he went out and "wept bitterly" (v. 62) after the rooster crowed and he realized that he had behaved just as Jesus said he would.

But despite Peter's "crime," God used him as one of the most influential leaders of the New Testament. It was Peter's powerful sermon on the Day of Shavuot (Pentecost) that led to the outpouring of the Spirit in the temple and the salvation of over three thousand people in one day.

In fact, look back through the list above and think about what some of these great "sinners" accomplished. Noah was the vessel through whom God saved the world during the time of the Flood. Moses freed the Israelites from slavery in Egypt. Abraham became the leader of a mighty nation—the nation through which the Messiah came into the world. David was a great king who was called a man after God's own heart. Solomon had the great privilege of building the temple, and is noted as one of the wisest men in all history.

And so it goes. Obviously, God's great mercy knows no bounds! In his book *The Furious Longing of God,* the late Brennan Manning writes:

> Jesus says, "Live in me. Make your home in me just as I do in you" (John 15:4, THE MESSAGE). Home is a place of welcoming love, nonjudgmental acceptance, accompanied by many signs of affection. His invitation to intimacy is startling.[1]

Manning goes on to quote the Apostle Paul. I'm going to quote him here in the Tree of Life Version:

> I pray that you, being rooted and grounded in love, may have strength to grasp with all the *kedoshim* what is the width and length and height and depth, and to know the

love of Messiah which surpasses knowledge, so you may
be filled up with all the fullness of God.

—Ephesians 3:17–19

HOW A HATER FOUND LOVE

Have you ever heard of a man named Thomas Tarrants? Talk
about someone who knows that God has a plan for his life.

Tom was born and raised in Alabama, and grew up in the
bloodiest days of the civil rights movement. He was a seg-
regationist who hated blacks and Jews, and believed that
Martin Luther King and other black leaders were pawns of the
Communist Party. As a teenager, Tarrants began reading racist
and anti-Semitic literature and became involved with the Ku
Klux Klan. His hatred knew no bounds, and he was absolutely
fearless. He began carrying out bombings of black churches
and Jewish businesses.

In 1968, Tom and another member of the Klan—a young
elementary schoolteacher by the name of Kathy Ainsworth—
planned to bomb the home of a successful Jewish businessman
in Meridian, Mississippi.

The FBI was waiting. Tarrants's partner died in a hail of
bullets. Tom was rushed to the hospital with four gunshot
wounds. He remembers lying on the ground, critically injured,
and hearing someone shout, "Shoot him! Shoot him!" The bullets that would have ended his life never came because people
had come pouring out of nearby houses to see what was going
on. Otherwise, Tom most certainly would have died that night.
Even so, doctors said it would be a miracle if he survived the
next hour.

But God had a plan for his life.

Against all odds, Tarrants survived, and he was sentenced to thirty years in the Mississippi State Penitentiary. Six months later, Tom and a group of other prisoners escaped.

One morning a few days later, Tom was "on guard duty" at the convicts' hideout when one of the other men relieved him a few minutes early. Almost as soon as Tom vacated his post, FBI sharpshooters opened fire. Tom's replacement was killed instantly.

Tom should have been dead—but God had a plan for his life.

Tom and the others were recaptured, and he spent the next three years in a six-by-nine-foot cell. He had plenty of time to read, and began with the same sort of literature that had spurred him to devote his life to hatred and violence.

Then he felt drawn to read the New Testament. Tom had read the Bible before, but always through the filter of his anger and hatred. This time it was different. Jesus's words of love, mercy, and tolerance pierced Tom to the heart. Even though he had been baptized as a teen, Tom hadn't really understood the significance of what he was doing, and had never sincerely surrendered his life to God. About his conversion, Tarrants wrote:

> I was overcome with a sense of my sinfulness—not just for prejudice, hatred, and political violence, but for my whole lifestyle. All my life I had been living for myself— what pleased me, made me feel good, made me look good to others. The feelings, needs, desires of other people were always secondary to what I wanted. Indeed, the whole world revolved around me and this showed itself in the outward sins of my life.
>
> As I came to see myself as I really was—as God saw me—I was crushed, and I wept bitterly. How hideous and wretched I was. Then, seeing my need so clearly and

knowing there was only One who could meet it, I surrendered myself to the Lord Jesus Christ as fully as I knew how. A tremendous weight was lifted from me, and I began to feel at peace at last.[2]

Tom Tarrants was a dangerous criminal who had been sentenced to life in prison without the possibility of parole. He was destined to spend the rest of his life behind bars.

But God had a plan for his life. After serving eight years of his sentence, Tom was pardoned. Release of such a dangerous, violent criminal was unheard of. But, like I said, God had plans for Tarrants's life.

He went to seminary and earned a degree in theology. He became pastor of an evangelical church in the Washington DC area, leading a flock noted for its racial diversity. He also served as president of the C. S. Lewis Society, an organization devoted to studying and propagating the thinking of one of the great Christian apologists of the twentieth century. Today, Tom is a gentle man who exudes love and kindness. It's almost impossible to think of him as the man who once carried out the violent orders of one of the most ruthless wings of the Ku Klux Klan.

But you see, God's plan for Tom Tarrants was to be a force for good and reconciliation. God's plans for us are always better than those we make for ourselves.

Do you ever feel condemned? I don't have to be a prophet to know that many of the people who read this book experience these feelings every day of their lives. We're all part of the human race, after all. But remember, God has a plan for every member of the human race, and that includes you.

Part of that plan is that if you confess your sins, He is faithful and just to forgive you. He will cleanse you from all unrighteousness and wipe the slate clean. (See 1 John 1:9.)

As you know, I'm from a Jewish family. I know what it is to be stiff-necked and rebellious. But God has been faithful to my people. He promised through Jeremiah, "As long as the sun shines by day and the moon and stars by night, they declare that I will preserve Israel as a nation, even though they have rejected me time and time again." (See Jeremiah 31:34–37.) I declare to you today that God is forgiving, and He is faithful. That guilt and condemnation you may be feeling are not from Him!

Don't Listen to Your Feelings

The problem with feeling forgotten, insignificant, or condemned is that feelings are often deceiving.

While feelings certainly do matter, they must always be subordinate to God's Word. Feelings may betray you, but the Word of God never will. The Word of God is the will of God. If God's Word says He cares about you, He does, even when you don't feel cared for. If God's Word says you are significant, then you are, even if you don't feel like it. If God's Word says you are forgiven and righteous, then you are forgiven and righteous, regardless of how unworthy you may feel. Let God be true and every man a liar! (See Romans 3:4.)

God says to us, "I know My plans for you. I know the destiny I have chosen for you. I know the calling that I've placed upon your life. That's why I revealed My Son to you. That's why I saved you. That's why I redeemed you. You have a purpose. This is the beginning, not the end."

When you accept the Lord and are born from above, it's the beginning of an exciting new life. But in order to enjoy God's plan for your future, you must shake off negative feelings and decide you're going to stand on the Word of God, regardless of how you feel.

At times, I've struggled with negative feelings that overwhelmed me. When this happens, I'll physically stand and look in the mirror and say over and over again to myself, "God has a plan for me! And it's a good plan!"

Jesus said that some people hear the Word of God but then "the worries of the world, the seduction of wealth, and the desires for other things enter in and choke the word, and it becomes unfruitful" (Mark 4:19).

I think that at one time or another most of us have been overly affected by "the worries of the world." We tend to focus on the difficult things that happen to us and forget about the blessings God gives us. I'm not pointing the finger at anyone. I just think this is human nature.

Think of what happened when Jesus healed the ten lepers in Luke 17, setting them free from disease and isolation and giving them hope for a bright future. Those ten men were as good as dead, but Jesus restored their hope and gave their lives back to them.

And yet only one of the ten came back to thank Jesus for the healing.

I believe that you'd be astounded if you could see how many times God intervenes for you every day. You'll never know the number of times you might have pulled into the path of an oncoming car, but He stopped you. How many times you might have tripped and fallen, but He caused you to change your path.

There are so many dangers lurking all around you and me, and He protects us from all of them. Our guardian angels are worn out and exhausted, and we aren't even aware that they've done anything to help us.

Learn to Expect Miracles

I believe most of us are far better at seeing the negative than the positive. We are constantly worried about life, and that colors everything. Is the government listening to our phone calls? Will the Internal Revenue Service decide to audit our tax returns? Where will terrorists strike today? Will the stock market crash? Will everything check out OK when we see the doctor next week?

And so it goes. I heard someone say that most people are either coming out of a storm, entering into a storm, or are right in the middle of a storm. And that seems to be true, doesn't it?

But God wants us to live in expectation of miracles, not in expectation of bad things! He doesn't want us to get out of bed in the morning and think, "I hope nothing bad happens to me today. I hope my tire doesn't go flat on the way to work. I hope the police don't give me a speeding ticket. I hope I don't fall and hurt myself." And so on.

Instead, God wants us to get out of bed in the morning with an excitement about what He's going to do in and through us today. We must start expecting miracles, because when we do, we'll experience them! If we expect bad stuff to happen, it will.

I am not one of those people who believe in a distorted "name it and claim it" faith theology. But I do believe that God expects us to put our faith into action. I am a strong advocate of biblical confession and walking in faith. The Bible says that when Jesus went back to His hometown of Nazareth, "He could not do any miracles there, except lay his hands on a few sick people and heal them. He was amazed at their lack of faith" (Mark 6:5–6, NIV). From this, I take it that our faith does play an important role in what we receive from God.

I also want to point out that the Bible is filled with promises from God to us, His people. It will help us so much if we can learn to focus on these promises rather than on the cares of the world. For example:

- "Therefore, there is now no condemnation for those who are in Messiah *Yeshua*" (Rom. 8:1).

- "But in all these things we are more than conquerors through Him who loved us" (Rom. 8:37).

- "He chose us in the Messiah before the foundation of the world, to be holy and blameless before Him in love. He predestined us for adoption as sons through Messiah Yeshua, in keeping with the good pleasure of His will—to the glorious praise of His grace, with which He favored us through the One He loves! In Him we have redemption through His blood—the removal of trespasses— in keeping with the richness of His grace that He lavished on us. In all wisdom and insight, He made known to us the mystery of His will, in keeping with His good pleasure that He planned in Messiah" (Eph. 1:4–9).

- "He rescued us from the domain of darkness and brought us into the kingdom of the Son whom He loves. In Him we have redemption—the release of sins" (Col. 1:13–14).

- "Therefore if anyone is in Messiah, he is a new creation. The old things have passed away; behold, all things have become new" (2 Cor. 5:17).

- "See how glorious a love the Father has given us, that we should be called God's children—and so we are!" (1 John 3:1).

C. S. Lewis, the great apologist and author of many classic works, wrote that he tried very hard in his younger years to be an atheist. One of his stated reasons for clinging to his doubt was that the universe seemed to be such a cruel and unjust place. But then he began to wonder how he had gotten the idea that something was cruel and unjust. What was the measuring stick he used? You can't really know what wrong is unless right exists. You can't know what sin is unless righteousness exists. You can't know what hate is unless love exists.

In *The Joyful Christian* Lewis wrote:

> A man does not call a line crooked unless he has some idea of a straight line. What was I comparing this universe with when I called it unjust? If the whole show was bad and senseless from A to Z, so to speak, why did I, who was supposed to be part of the show, find myself in such violent reaction against it? A man feels wet when he falls into water, because man is not a water animal: a fish would not feel wet. Of course, I could have given up my idea of justice by saying it was nothing but a private idea of my own. But if I did that, then my argument against God collapsed too—for the argument depended on saying that the world was really unjust, not simply that it did not happen to please my private fancies. Thus in the very act of trying to prove that God did not exist—in other words, that the whole of reality was senseless—I found I was forced to assume that one part of reality—namely my idea of justice—was full of sense. Consequently atheism turns out to be too simple. If the whole universe has no meaning, we should never have

found out that it has no meaning: just as, if there were no light in the universe and therefore no creatures with eyes, we should never know it was dark. *Dark* would be without meaning.[3]

C. S. Lewis discovered that there is right and love in the universe. As the Apostle John writes in 1 John 4:16, "God is love." In fact, God loves us more than we can possibly understand.

Not long ago I heard a story about a believer who was on her way somewhere in her car when she had a clear impression that she was supposed to stop at a convenience store. She pulled into the parking lot, turned off the engine, and sat there with her heart pounding. Was God really speaking to her, or had her imagination got the best of her?

After a moment, to her great surprise, she got the idea that she was supposed to go into that store, do a handstand against the wall, and call out to the clerk, "Look what I can do!"

No! That was dumb. She wasn't going to do anything like that.

She started the car and began to drive away.

But as she did, the feeling became even stronger, and she wondered, was she willing to make a fool of herself if God wanted her to?

She pulled back into her parking space, waited a few more minutes, and then got out and made her way into the store. There were a couple of customers in there, so she spent some time browsing among the soda pop and potato chips, trying to get up her courage and waiting for them to leave.

Finally, the others paid for their purchases and exited the store. There was nobody in there but her and the clerk—a young man in his midtwenties. It was now or never!

She hurried to the wall, flipped into a handstand, and shouted, "Look what I can do!"

Then she scrambled back to her feet and prepared to make her escape before the clerk had a chance to call the police.

To her surprise, a tear trickled down his cheek. Then he lowered his head and began to sob.

"What's the matter?" she asked.

He explained that he had been going through a terrible time. His life was such a mess that he was barely hanging on to his faith.

That morning he had challenged God to prove His existence. "If You're really there, I want You to send someone into the store and have them stand on their head."

Now, I'm not saying that God will respond to every prayer like that one. He is under no obligation to go around proving that He exists. But He knows people's hearts and is willing to go to great lengths to show us how much He loves us—and He has a great sense of humor!

In his million-selling classic, *They Speak with Other Tongues*, John Sherrill tells of another occasion when God took unusual steps to prove Himself. It happened during the Azusa Street Revival in Los Angeles during the early 1900s. That revival is known as the birthplace of the modern Pentecostal movement.

Sherrill writes, "The Azusa Street Revival lasted for three years. Rich and poor alike came to see what was going on. People came from nearby towns, from the Midwest, from New England, Canada, Great Britain. There were whites and African-Americans, old and young, educated and illiterate. Reporters from all over the country came to investigate, and whether they filed reports that were favorable or unfavorable, they always had a good story."[4]

Sherrill got this story from a man named Harvey McAlister:

My brother, Robert E. McAlister, now deceased, was in Los Angeles when the following incident took place and he reported it to me. The girl, whom I knew intimately, and I heard the incident also from her parents, was Kathleen Scott...

There was a large auditorium with an "Upper Room" upstairs. The place was open day and night for several years, with preaching services two or three times daily, and people in prayer in the Upper Room day and night... When time came for preaching, someone would ring a bell and all would come downstairs for the services.

Kathleen was in the Upper Room, teen-age, at this particular time. A man entered the building, the service now being in process, and hearing people pray, he ventured upstairs to the prayer room. The moment he entered, Kathleen, moved by the Spirit, arose and pointed to the man...and spoke in a language other than her own for several minutes.

The ringing of the bell, calling the people to the preaching service, interrupted. All the people arose and made their way to the stairway. The man, as Kathleen approached the stairs, took her arm and directed her downstairs, to the speaker's desk and waited until order was restored in the auditorium. Then he spoke.

"I am a Jew, and I came to this city to investigate this speaking in tongues. No person in this city knows my first or my last name, as I am here under an assumed name. No one in this city knows my occupation, or anything about me. I go to hear preachers for the purpose of taking their sermons apart, and using them in lecturing against the Christian religion.

"This girl, as I entered the room, started speaking in the Hebrew language. She told me my first name and my last name, and she told me why I was in the city and what my occupation was in life, and then she...told me things about my life which it would impossible for any person in this city to know."

Then [Mr. McAlister's letter concludes], the man dropped to his knees and cried and prayed as though his heart would break.[5]

Brennan Manning, whom I quoted earlier in this chapter, has much to say about God's love in his best-selling book, *Abba's Child*.

God is relentlessly tender and compassionate toward us just as we are—not in spite of our sins and faults (that would not be total acceptance), but with them. Though God does not condone or sanction evil, He does not withhold His love because there is evil in us.[6]

Just a few pages later Manning quotes Thomas Merton, who wrote:

God loves you, is present in you, lives in you, dwells in you, calls you, saves you, and offers you an understanding and compassion which are like nothing you have ever found in a book or heard in a sermon.[7]

"I'LL NEVER FILL HIS SHOES"

I will never forget the wonderful way God confirmed His plan for me at a time when I became discouraged and felt that I could no longer continue leading Jewish Voice. I had recently taken over for the former president and founder, Louis Kaplan, who had gone on to be with the Lord. He was a pioneer and healing evangelist God used powerfully during the healing revivals in the late 1940s and 1950s. He founded Jewish Voice Broadcast back in 1967 right before the Six-Day War broke out, and he led the ministry for over three decades until he suffered a debilitating stroke in 1997 and passed away a year later.

For the first few months, everything had gone great. The people loved me, I loved them, and I seemed to be a great fit. But the all-too-brief honeymoon had now come to an end, and I seemed to experience resistance from my staff at every turn. I constantly heard, "That's not how Brother K did it," or, "That's not how we do it around here." I couldn't seem to do anything right. Finally, I was fed up. I'd had it!

Kaplan's widow, Chira, invited me to dinner, and I proceeded to unload my frustrations on her. I told her I was ready to quit. "I can't do this anymore," I said. "I'll never be able to fill Brother Kaplan's shoes."

As I spoke those words, Chira jumped up as if she'd suddenly remembered something important. "That reminds me," she exclaimed, "I have something for you. I meant to give it to you before, but I forgot."

She disappeared into her bedroom and came out a minute or so later carrying three shoeboxes—each with a brand-new pair of Florsheim shoes—shoes that Louis Kaplan had purchased but had never worn.

Now, it so happens that I have a very unusual shoe size—8½ EEE. Guess what size they were? That's right, 8½ EEE. To this day (although one pair wore down until the heels had holes in them and I had to get rid of them) they remain the most comfortable shoes I own!

God has such a sense of humor. Under my own power, my own ability, and my own strength, I was inadequate. But through the Lord's power, because of His calling on my life, I *could* fill Brother Kaplan's shoes. I *do* fill Brother Kaplan's shoes. Through God's grace, because this was His plan for me,

I have now been leading the ministry for over eighteen years. During that time we have seen unprecedented growth—from fifteen on staff to over one hundred—and a budget thirty times greater than it was when I took over the ministry!

I learned some great lessons from this. One of the most important is, "Don't say, 'No, I can't,' when God says, 'Yes, you can!'"

IF GOD SAYS IT, BELIEVE IT

I want you to know that you can absolutely trust God. If He says something, you can take it to the bank. And what He says to you is that He loves you, has a plan for your life, and wants to give you hope and a future.

The Bible is just one of the places we can go to find verification of God's reliability. If the Bible was sloppy in the details we can double-check, then we might be tempted to question its authority in spiritual matters. Instead, the more we know about history, geography, and anthropology, the more impressed we are by the Bible's meticulous accuracy.

There you have it. As the Bible itself says: "Those who know Your Name trust You—for You, ADONAI, have never forsaken those who seek You" (Ps. 9:11).

Chapter 4

UNDERSTANDING GOD'S PLAN FOR YOUR LIFE

*The heavens declare the glory of God; the skies
proclaim the work of his hands.*

—PSALM 19:1, NIV

O UR VERY SURVIVAL depends on God's precision. The more we know about this world we live in, the more we can see that His grace and mercy are all around us. We truly are "fearfully and wonderfully made" (Ps. 139:14, NIV), and the universe we live in is every bit as remarkable.

For example, if the earth were not tilted at an angle of twenty-three degrees, the entire planet would be covered with ice. And if the earth's crust were ten feet thicker, there would be no oxygen in our atmosphere—and thus no animal life would be possible. Scientists also tell us that if the oceans were just a few feet deeper, all carbon dioxide and oxygen would be absorbed into them, meaning that no animals *or* plants could survive on the planet.

Furthermore, the earth is the exact distance from the sun necessary to sustain life. A few million miles closer and we'd all burn up. A few million miles in the other direction and we'd freeze to death. Clearly, none of these things is mere coincidence.

In his book *Soul Survivor* Philip Yancey quotes a physicist named Chet Raymo. Although Raymo does not believe in a Creator, he says:

> If, one second after the Big Bang, the ratio of the density of the universe to its expansion rate had differed from its assumed value by only one part in 10^{15}, (that's 1 followed by fifteen zeroes), the universe would have either quickly collapsed upon itself or ballooned so rapidly that stars and galaxies could not have condensed from the primal matter… The coin was flipped into the air 10^{15} times, and it came down on its edge but once. If all the grains of sand on all the beaches of the Earth were possible universes—that is, universes consistent

with the laws of physics as we know them—and only one of those grains of sand were a universe that allowed for the existence of intelligent life, then that one grain of sand is the universe we inhabit.[1]

How could he *not* be a believer?

All of these things show us how precise God was when He created the universe. He thought of absolutely everything necessary for human life to survive and thrive. In other words, He designed this world with you and me in mind. He gave us air to breathe, water to drink, food to eat, and sleep and exercise to restore our bodies. When we see what He has done for us in this way, it's even easier to believe and trust Him when He says, "For I know the plans I have for you, plans to prosper you and not to harm you, plans to give you hope and a future."

If a look at the earth isn't enough to convince anyone that we have a loving Creator who thinks of every detail we need to live and thrive, let's lower our sights a little bit—to an insect. More precisely, to the honeybee.

Did you know that worker bees will sometimes fly several miles looking for a good source of pollen? Once one of the bees has found what he's looking for, he flies all the way back to his home hive and tells the other bees all about it. How does he do this? By performing a dance with a complicated series of gyrations. One of his movements lets the other bees know which direction to travel. Another lets them know how far they'll have to travel. And a third dance step lets the other bees know the size and scope of the find.

All of this from a simple insect.

And then, of course, there's also the honey, which is nutritious and delicious too.

And how about the human body?

Did you know that if all the blood vessels in your body were laid end to end, they would stretch for more than sixty thousand miles? That's enough to go around the earth twice, with more than ten thousand miles left over! Every day these blood vessels are busy carrying blood to trillions of cells throughout your body. That's trillion with a "t." And yet these cells work in complete unity and harmony to carry out your body's necessary functions.

Think about the human brain. It enables you to think, hear, smell, taste, see, and do hundreds of other functions that you don't even have to spend time thinking about. It is much more complex than the fastest, most advanced computer, but it is completely "natural." When I think of all the functions that are handled by the brain, I think of what it must be like for a television director at the Summer Olympics. Let me explain.

Every four years, the world gets a chance to watch the Olympic Games on television. As much as I'm amazed by the power, grace, and skill of those young athletes from all over the world, I'm just as impressed by the skill of the person who's sitting in the director's chair in the TV studio control room.

He or she has to quickly select from one camera shot to the next in a way that seems continuous to the viewing audience and presents the most interesting way of telling the story. Camera one shows a tight close-up of a determined face. Cut to camera two for a wide shot of the playing field. Quick! Back to camera three to catch that shot on goal. There are so many choices to make—and even more when you take into account the number of sporting events that are taking place simultaneously. You have to decide where the action is—whether it's on the basketball court, the soccer field, the track, and so on—and make sure you stay on top of it. That's the type of action your brain is involved in every instant of the day. It tells the heart to beat, orders the lungs to breathe, and commands the stomach to digest food. These are just some of the amazing things that happen in the human body every single day, and all under the direction of that amazing computer God created many thousands of years ago—the human brain.

All of these things are indicative of a God who is intimately involved and active with His creation, a God who cares. In the Sermon on the Mount Jesus said:

> Look at the birds of the air. They do not sow or reap or gather into barns; yet your Father in heaven feeds them. Are you not of more value than they? And which of you by worrying can add a single hour to his life? And why do you worry about clothing? Consider the lilies of the field, how they grow. They neither toil nor spin…Now if in this way God clothes the grass—which is here today and thrown into the furnace tomorrow—will He not much more clothe you, O you of little faith? Therefore do not worry, saying, "What will we eat?" or "What will we drink?" or "What will we wear?" For the pagans eagerly pursue all these things; yet your Father in heaven knows that you need all these. But seek first the kingdom of God and His righteousness, and all these things shall be added to you.
>
> —MATTHEW 6:26–33

God not only has a plan for you, but He wants to prosper you. Please understand that when the Lord says He wants to prosper us, He is not necessarily using the word as the world defines it. When we think of prosperity from the world's perspective, we think of having a bigger and better car, a nicer house, wealth and worldly riches. More, more, more. But that is not what biblical prosperity is about. The Hebrew word translated "prosperity" is *shalom*. Allow me to expand on this further in the next chapter.

Chapter 5

GOD'S PLANS TO PROSPER YOU

*"For I know the plans I have for you," declares the
Lord, "plans to prosper you and not to harm you."*

—JEREMIAH 29:11, NIV, EMPHASIS ADDED

*I will surely make you prosper and will make your descendants
like the sand of the sea, which cannot be counted.*

—GENESIS 32:12, NIV

With me are wealth and honor, enduring riches and righteousness.

—PROVERBS 8:18

I REMEMBER HOW SURPRISED I was when I first studied Jeremiah 29:11 in the original Hebrew. Unexpectedly, I discovered that the Hebrew word translated as "prosper" in the NIV, "welfare" in the Revised Standard Version and other translations, and "peace" in the King James and New King James Versions is *shalom* (שלום).

Shalom is a great Hebrew word. It's like *aloha* in Hawaiian. It can mean hello, and it can also mean good-bye. In Israel, if you don't know whether you're coming or going, just say, "Shalom." It works either way!

Shalom also means peace. On Shabbat, or as Shabbat is approaching, we Jews greet one another by saying "Shabbat Shalom," which means "Sabbath peace." We are exhorted in Psalm 122:6 to "pray for the peace of Jerusalem." Again, the Hebrew word is *shalom*. One of the names of Yeshua is *Sar Shalom*, the Prince of Peace.

Shalom also means wellness, well-being, happiness, welfare, prosperity, health, rest, and wholeness. I believe the best and fullest definition of the word is "to complete or bring to completion." Shalom is one of the richest words in the Hebrew language.

Two scriptures I believe capture this idea of shalom best are, "In Him you have been made complete, and He is the head over all rule and authority" (Col. 2:10, NAS), and "Let perseverance finish its work so that you may be mature and complete, not lacking anything" (James 1:4, NIV).

Let me go back for a moment to Psalm 122:6, "Pray for the peace (shalom) of Jerusalem," which just so happens to be one of my favorite scriptures. People ask me all the time, "How should we deal with the Middle East situation as Christians?

How should we pray for Israel? Should there be a Palestinian state? Can there be peace? Should we pray for the 'road map' and human efforts to end the conflict?"

When we are exhorted to pray for the shalom of Jerusalem, we are not just to pray for peace, we are to pray for His *completion*, for His plans and purposes to be fulfilled for both the land and the people of Israel.

I believe there is only one workable "peace plan" for the Middle East, and that is the "Prince of Peace," Yeshua, Jesus the Messiah. He is the only way Jew and Arab will find peace and learn to live together as brothers and sisters.

When God says, "My plan for you is to prosper you," He is saying that He wants to pour out His shalom on you. He wants you to walk in His well-being. He wants you to rest in His rest and experience His peace that passes all understanding. God is expressing His desire to bring you into His completion and into His fullness.

Jesus said, "I have come that they [you] might have life, and have it abundantly!" (John 10:10). And, "Come to Me, all you who are weary and burdened, and I will give you rest. Take My yoke upon you and learn from Me, for I am gentle and humble in heart, and 'you will find rest for your souls.' For My yoke is easy and My burden is light" (Matt. 11:28–30).

Prosperity is not about the need to accumulate everything we possibly can. That is selfishness and greed, pure and simple. He promises to meet every *need*, not *greed*. Rather, prosperity is coming to a place of completeness in God, where everything we desire is His desire, and everything He desires is our desire. And when we desire the same things He desires, everything we ask will come to pass because it's His will.

Do you see the difference? Let's not fall into the trap of the so-called American dream, the false notion that success is defined by having bigger and better, the best of everything. That's not what God wants for us, nor should it be what we want for ourselves.

I actually heard one prosperity teacher tell his audience, "Right now, you may have only enough faith to drive a Ford or a Chevy. But as your faith increases, you'll be able to move up to a Cadillac or a Mercedes." I'm not sure I've used his exact words, but I've certainly captured the gist of what he said. And I find absolutely nothing in the Bible that teaches that God will indulge our greed in this way. We have His guarantee that He will give us everything we need to live life to the fullest—but my own experience tells me that the closer we get to God, the fewer material things we long for. The more we touch His heart, the more we understand that everything He gives us, He gives with other people in mind.

Remember that when the rich young ruler asked Jesus what he needed to do to gain eternal life, Jesus replied, "Go, sell as much as you have, and give to the poor; and you will have treasure in heaven. Then come, follow Me" (Mark 10:21). He did not say, "Come follow me, and I'll give you eternal life, plus I'll make you twice as rich as you are right now." So often our possessions get in the way of our relationship with God, as was the case with the young ruler, who went away sad when he heard these words because he had great wealth and that wealth had such control over him that he was not able to follow the Lord.

It's never enough when you get caught up in materialism. There is always something bigger, better, or more expensive out there. And just when you think you've arrived, your neighbor gets something that you just have to have too. As they say, the grass is always greener on the other side of the fence.

Yes, I believe in prosperity—but I believe in biblical prosperity, a completeness in Him that fills the void in our lives that He and He alone can fill.

GOD ALWAYS INTENDED FOR US TO PROSPER

From the very beginning of creation, God intended for His people to prosper and live in peace and harmony with one another and with nature. But that all changed when Satan, in the form of a serpent, tempted the first man and woman to disobey God in the Garden of Eden.

Everything was perfect before that tragic event brought sin, death, evil, and poverty into the world. Just think about it. Before sin came, human beings never went hungry, never experienced sickness, never knew what it was to be depressed, exhausted, or ashamed. God was there to provide everything they needed and desired.

They lived in perfect harmony with the other creatures God had made. The animals did not have a natural fear of mankind. Birds didn't fly away at the first sound of a human voice. Squirrels and rabbits waited to be petted when Adam and Eve came near. So did lions and tigers. Were there dinosaurs in those days? I don't know. But if there were, I know they were friendly. In that respect, I believe the world was like a fantasy movie.

The Bible even tells us that God brought the animals He had created to Adam so Adam could name them. (See Genesis 2:19–20.) I believe that says something very special about mankind's relationship with the other animals.

But obviously, it's not that way anymore.

Do you ever watch those *National Geographic* wildlife specials on television? They are beautifully filmed and extremely entertaining—but I have trouble watching them. Why? Because I know that sooner or later, that cute little zebra is going to become a hungry lion's dinner. The playful seal will be gobbled up by a killer whale. And the adorable meerkat is likely to fall prey to a python or rattlesnake.

This is how it is in nature: kill or be killed, survival of the fittest. But this is all the result of sin. God never intended the world to be this way.

Before sin came into the world, the first humans had an intimate and perfect relationship with God. They walked and talked with Him in the garden in the cool of the evening. They had no doubts, fears, or worries. They had plenty of food to eat. They never had a sore throat or a headache. The weather was always perfect. They were like joyful children who knew that their strong Father would never let any harm come to them. Actually, they didn't even know what "harm" was because they had never experienced it—although it was lurking nearby in the form of a serpent.

In the days before the fall of man, the whole universe was living in a state of shalom. Everything happened when and how it was supposed to, like clockwork. All was predictable, but it was never boring or monotonous. Life was an unending cycle of peace, joy, and prosperity.

The sun came up in the morning. The moon and stars came out at night. A mist went up from the ground and watered all the plants. Adam and Eve never even experienced a rainy day.

God intended human beings to be the kings and queens of creation. The Bible says, "God blessed them and God said to them, 'Be fruitful and multiply, fill the land, and conquer it. Rule over the fish of the sea, the flying creatures of the sky, and over every animal that crawls on the land'" (Gen. 1:28).

The author of Genesis also tells us that when God had finished His work of creating, He looked over what He had done, "and behold it was very good" (Gen. 1:31).

Cornelius Plantinga, former present of Calvin Theological Seminary, writes:

> The webbing together of God, humans, and all creation in justice, fulfillment, and delight is what the Hebrew prophets called *shalom*. We call it "peace," but it means far more than just peace of mind or cease-fire among enemies (As a matter of fact, the area over which two armies declare a cease-fire may be acres of smoldering ruin.). In the Bible, shalom means universal flourishing, wholeness, and delight—a rich state of affairs in which natural needs are satisfied and natural gifts fruitfully employed, all under the arch of God's love. Shalom, in other words, is the way things are supposed to be.[1]

Then Satan came into the picture and made a mess of everything. Shalom went from being an everyday reality to an elusive shadowy substance, something America's founding fathers called "the pursuit of happiness."

When Adam and Eve fell into sin, God told them:

> Cursed is the ground because of you—with pain will you eat of it all the days of your life. Thorns and thistles will sprout for you. You will eat the plants of the field. By the sweat of your brow will you eat food, until you return to the ground, since from it were you taken. For you are dust, and to dust will you return.
> —Genesis 3:17–19

When Adam and Eve submitted to Satan, they turned over to him the power that was rightfully theirs. Another way to look at it is that they handed him the title deed to the world we live in. Thousands of years later, when Yeshua came to earth as a human being, Satan tried the same trick on Him. But this time—praise God!—it didn't work.

The Book of Matthew says that after Yeshua was baptized by John, He went into the desert, where He fasted for forty days and was tempted by Satan. Satan was doing his best to get Him to sin so that He would no longer be fit to fulfill His role as Messiah of Israel and Savior of mankind.

Matthew writes in chapter four of his Gospel that in one of these temptations, the devil took Him to the top of a very high mountain, showed Him all the kingdoms of the world and their splendor, and said, "All these things I will give You, if You fall down and worship me" (Matt. 4:9).

Yeshua responded by quoting Scripture, and reminding Satan that God alone is to be worshipped. But He did not say, "You can't give Me what doesn't belong to you." All of these kingdoms had indeed been handed over to Satan by Adam and Eve when they disobeyed God and ate of the forbidden fruit. That's precisely why Jesus had come into the world—to pay the debt for our sin and restore everything to the way it was always supposed to be. In other words, He came to restore the state of "shalom" that existed prior to mankind's fall in the garden.

Three times in the Book of John, Yeshua refers to Satan as the prince or ruler of this world. Two of those times He says that Satan has been judged or defeated.

- "Now is the judgment of this world! Now the prince of this world will be driven out!" (John 12:31).

- "I will not talk with you much longer, for the ruler of this world is coming. He has nothing on Me. But in order that the world may know that I love the Father, I do exactly as the Father commanded Me" (John 14:30–31).

- "The ruler of this world has been judged" (John 16:11).

Satan has been defeated, and the day will yet come when he is destroyed completely. Right now he is like a mortally wounded beast, trying to take as many people as possible down with him, and our world still bears the wounds and scars of his savagery and cruelty. Somehow he thinks he can still hang on to control and evade the ultimate death sentence, the "crushing of his head." (See Genesis 3:15.)

That's why we have so much trouble in this world. That's why we turn on the news and see heartbreaking reports about the brutality inflicted on innocent people by Islamic State terrorists. That's why many millions of people are living in terrible poverty, without enough to eat, clean water, proper shelter, or access to basic medicines. It's why so many people are still dying every day from diseases like cancer, despite the billions of dollars that have been poured into defeating them. That is the reason that bad things happen to good people.

As someone has said, "Satan is still alive and well on planet Earth."

Actually, though, that's not completely true. Satan is not "well," even though that may be the impression we get when we watch the evening news. He was defeated when Jesus rose from the dead on that Sunday morning nearly two thousand years ago. His destruction is certain. The Book of Revelation tells us that when the end times have come, Satan will "come out to deceive the nations at the four corners of the earth, Gog and Magog, to gather them for the battle. Their number is like the sand of the sea. And they came up on the broad plain of the earth and surrounded the camp of the *kedoshim* (holy ones) and the beloved city—but fire fell from heaven and consumed them. And the devil who deceived them was thrown into the lake of fire and brimstone, where the beast and the false prophet are too, and they shall be tortured day and night forever and ever" (Rev. 20:8–10).

Prosperity Is Coming for All

A day is coming when the whole world will once again experience shalom as God intended. Isaiah says:

> The wolf will dwell with the lamb, the leopard will lie down with the kid, the calf and the young lion and the yearling together, and a little child will lead them. The cow and the bear will graze, their young ones lie down together, and the lion will eat straw like an ox. A nursing child will play by a cobra's hole, and a weaned child will put his hand into a viper's den. They will not hurt or destroy in all My holy mountain, for the earth will be full of the knowledge of Adonai, as the waters cover the sea.
>
> —Isaiah 11:6–9

I love this beautiful picture of the world's future. But the really good news is that those who believe in and belong to the Lord can experience inner contentment and prosperity right now as they walk in faith and obedience.

The Bible refers to Jesus as "the last Adam." The fifteenth chapter of 1 Corinthians says, "For as in Adam all die, so in

Christ all will be made alive" (v. 22, NIV). Paul goes on to write, "So also it is written, 'The first man, Adam, became a living soul.' The last Adam became a life-giving spirit. However, the spiritual is not first, but the natural; then the spiritual. The first man is of the earth, made of dust; the second man is from heaven. Like the one made of dust, so also are those made of dust; and like the heavenly, so also are those who are heavenly. And just as we have borne the image of the one made from dust, so also shall we bear the image of the One from heaven" (vv. 45–49).

Believers are to bear the Messiah's image, not only in heaven but also here on earth. Jesus said, "Amen, amen I tell you, he who puts his trust in Me, the works that I do he will do; and greater than these he will do, because I am going to the Father. And whatever you ask in My name, that I will do, so that the Father may be glorified in the Son. If you ask Me anything in My name, I will do it" (John 14:12–14).

Let me repeat myself as I close this chapter. A day is coming when Satan and his followers will be removed from the picture. When that happens, all evil will disappear. There will be no more suffering, sickness, tears, poverty, death, or pain of any kind. The Book of Revelation says that God will wipe every tear from our eyes. (See Revelation 7:17; 21:4.) What a glorious day that will be!

But until that day comes, God promises that we, His children, can have a foretaste of the divine prosperity He has always intended for His creation. As we grow closer to Him through spending time in His presence, hearing His voice, and obeying His Word, we are conformed more and more into the image of His Son. As that happens, we experience true shalom—a completion and fulfillment found only in Him.

As Paul writes:

> I have been crucified with Messiah; and it is no longer I who live, but Messiah lives in me. And the life I now live in the body, I live by trusting in Ben-Elohim [the Son of God]—who loved me and gave Himself up for me.
>
> —GALATIANS 2:20

Chapter 6

GOD WILL KEEP YOU FROM HARM

"For I know the plans I have for you," declares the
LORD, *"plans to prosper you and not to harm you."*

—JEREMIAH 29:11, NIV, EMPHASIS ADDED

GOD'S PLAN FOR us *never* includes the infliction of harm. This includes harm in all forms—moral, physical, or psychological. He always wants what's best for us, not what will cause us pain, hardship, or suffering. The Tree of Life version of the Scriptures translates the words above from Jeremiah 29:11 as, "plans for shalom and not calamity."

THE HEBREW WORD FOR HARM— OR CALAMITY—IS *RA*

Ra (רע) means bad or evil. Its meaning encompasses all forms of evil.

In English Bibles *ra* is most commonly translated as "evil" or "wicked." But it also conveys something that has been spoiled and is no longer good for anything—physically, socially, or morally. It is the word we would use for fruit that has become overripe and is no good for anything except to be thrown away. Yeshua used this analogy in Matthew 5:13 when He said, "You are the salt of the earth; but if the salt should lose its flavor, how shall it be made salty again? It is no longer good for anything, except to be thrown out and trampled under foot by men."

A MATTER OF PERSPECTIVE

There have been some times in my life when I wondered why God "failed" to answer one of my desperate prayers, or when I thought He let me down by not giving me something I felt I needed. I've prayed for many people who have not been healed. I've watched tragedy befall "good people" who love God. I've lost friends and family to terminal illnesses and wonder why God did not intervene or why He allowed them to suffer. In those times, it often feels like God did not fulfill His promise in Jeremiah 29.

But in hindsight I realize that I was looking at the situation from a short-term, earthly perspective, whereas God sees things from an eternal, heavenly perspective. Because of our spiritual myopia, we are not always able to understand His divine purposes when we feel like He has failed us.

As we've already seen, the people of Israel had been forcibly relocated to Babylon when Jeremiah gave them God's promise that His plans for them did not include harm. Some of the people who heard this message must have found it ironic, wondering how anything could be more harmful than being conquered by another nation, and how anything good could possibly come out of their situation.

And yet this time in Israel's history was:

> ...Marked by a resurgence in Jewish traditions, as the exiles looked back to their Mosaic origins in an effort to revive their original religion. It is most likely the Torah took its final shape during this period or shortly afterward, and that it became the central text of the Jewish faith at this time as well.

> During this period, Jewish leaders no longer spoke about a theology of judgment, but a theology of salvation.[1]

The Jews in Babylon couldn't look beyond their temporary predicament to see the longtime good that would come from it. They would be brought together as a people. Their faith would be strengthened. The Torah would take shape. Although their exile to Babylon was the result of their own sin and disobedience, and God warned them over and over this would happen if they did not change their ways, God brought blessing out of their adversity. This is exactly what He promises to do for us. "And we know that in all things God works for the good of those who love him, who have been called according to his purpose" (Rom. 8:28, NIV). Not only does God promise not to inflict harm upon us, but even when we get into trouble as a result of our own sin, disobedience, or stupidity, He has an amazing way of bringing good things out of it. He blesses us even in the midst of our own mistakes.

Some people seem to have the idea that God is always looking for a reason to throw lightning bolts at them. They picture Him as a police officer with a billy club who is ready to bop them over the head, or an angry old schoolmaster, like someone from a Charles Dickens novel, going around with a big scowl on His face, just daring anybody to do something that makes Him angry.

But that's certainly not who the God of the Bible is. It's not the heavenly Father I've come to know. The Jewish calendar is full of *moedim* (appointed days, feasts, or festivals) when God has called His people to come together to celebrate with Him. As the word *feast* suggests, most of those days include lots of good food, celebration, and rejoicing. Our God loves to party. He loves when we enjoy life.

The Bible depicts God as the loving Father who joyfully comes running to meet the prodigal son or daughter returning to Him after years of rebellion. He is the one who says, "Bring the fattened calf and kill it! Let's celebrate with a feast! For this son of mine was dead and has come back to life—he was lost and is found!" (Luke 15:23–24). He wants His people to thrive, not to live in constant fear and dread.

GOD NEVER CAUSES SIN

One of the many things God means when He says He will not harm you is that He will not cause you to sin. I pastored a congregation for nine years, and I can't even begin to count the number of people who came to me during that time with—and here's another Hebrew word for you: *meshugenah* revelations—crazy ideas of what God wanted for them. A number of unhappy husbands and wives said they felt certain that God had told them they should divorce. I've heard these exact words countless times: "God showed me I'm to get divorced because He wants me to be happy."

There's only one problem with that, and it's a big one. The Bible says that God hates divorce (Mal. 2:16). Jesus verified that when He said, "Because of your hardness of heart Moses permitted you to divorce your wives, but from the beginning it was not so. Now I tell you, whoever divorces his wife, except for sexual immorality, and marries another, commits adultery" (Matt. 19:8–9). Yes, God wants you to be happy in marriage, not by divorce but through reconciliation and restoration.

I once heard the testimony of an ex-drug dealer who had gone back into dealing drugs because he believed the Lord wanted him to raise money for a new building for his church through his drug sales!

As I've already shared, I absolutely believe God has a way of working things together for good even when you mess up. He *will* redeem your life when you repent. And God *will* allow you to sin if you give in to your flesh. But this is a very different thing than God *causing* you to sin for some divine purpose. God will never *cause* you to sin for *any* reason. That is completely against His nature and His plan for your life.

Yes, God can bring good out of anything, including our biggest moral failures. But it is never His intent for us to do anything harmful—for any reason. God will never violate His Word. And because we know this is true, we can also know that He will never cause us to sin or tempt us to sin.

The Book of James says:

> Let no one say when he is tempted, "I am being tempted by God"—for God cannot be tempted by evil, and He himself tempts no one. But each one is tempted when he is dragged away and enticed by his own desire. Then when desire has conceived, it gives birth to sin; and when sin is full grown, it brings forth death.
>
> —James 1:13–15

Sin is sin. It comes from the temptation of this world. It comes from the carnal mind, the flesh. It comes from Satan, the enemy of our souls. Never from God.

Not only will God not cause you to sin, He will not strike you with calamity. Sometimes people ask, "Why did God give me this disease?" The truth is that sickness and bad things happen to good people because we live in a world that still has to overcome death. We are still suffering from the sin that Adam and Eve committed in the Garden of Eden, when they disobeyed God and ate from the tree of the knowledge of good and evil. We live in a fallen world.

The Bible says, "The last enemy to be destroyed is death" (1 Cor. 15:26). Although *we* are redeemed, we live in a *world* that has not yet been redeemed. That is the difficult reality. It is why we have to be in Him. It is in Him that we find healing, health, wholeness, and life. The world is decaying, sick, and dying, but God did not bring these calamities upon us.

As Jesus told His disciples:

> Abide in Me, and I will abide in you. The branch cannot itself produce fruit, unless it abides on the vine. Likewise, you cannot produce fruit unless you abide in Me. I am the vine; you are the branches. The one who abides in Me, and I in him, bears much fruit; for apart from Me, you can do nothing.
>
> —JOHN 15:4–5

God will allow difficult things to come to us as a consequence for what we do. Still, He is not the cause of these difficulties. How do I know this? Because the Hebrew word *ra* includes moral, physical, and spiritual dimensions. God includes nothing harmful in His plan for you and me, and that means He doesn't cause sickness or other personal tragedies. We live in a world where sickness abounds. That too is the result of sin. But we also have a Bible that promises us, "By His stripes we are healed" (Isa. 53:5)!

Terry McGonigal, Dean of Spiritual Life at Whitworth University, writes, "Evil (*ra'*) is one [of] the most pervasive terms in the [Old Testament], appearing 310 times." He adds that *ra* "is the antonym of shalom, the antithesis of all that God desired and still intends for all creation."[2]

McGonigal paints a poignant picture of what happened when *ra* entered God's creation. This occurred when the serpent convinced Adam and Eve to eat fruit that God had commanded them to avoid. In fact, He had told them that eating the fruit would bring an extremely severe penalty: death. And yet they ate it anyway.

As McGonigal explains, the first negative thing that came into the world through *ra* was shame. Then came separation.

Human beings were separated from their God, fearing Him and hiding from Him. Men and women were separated from each other, pointing fingers at each other and blaming each other instead of accepting responsibility for their own actions.

Dr. McGonigal paints a vivid picture of how *ra* changed creation: "At the end of the creation process, 'God saw everything that God had made, and indeed, it was very good' (*tov me'od*) [in Hebrew]. Like an artist after the last brushstroke, [the] Creator rejoices in the outcome. God delights in creation's splendor ablaze with color....God scans the earth, three quarters covered with water; majestic seas and meandering streams, tiny ponds and lakes so big they look like oceans, rushing rivers that course through landscape for thousands of miles. God rejoices with all of creation saturated in abundant life...According to God's design, each and every part of creation is distinct, interconnected and interdependent. God's separating-binding process results in creation's distinctiveness and connection: *shalom beauty*."[3]

But then, "*Shalom* does not last long. The biblical framing story describes how things got the way they are now, 'not the way it's supposed to be.' A violent assault upon God's *shalom* takes place, and every part of the web is changed. Within a few chapters God's *shalom* becomes so polluted that the original web is nearly unrecognizable and its memory almost gone."[4]

Satan had promised Adam and Eve that when they ate of the forbidden fruit, they would become wise, like God. But wisdom was not the first thing they experienced. Instead, the first thing they experienced was shame. They were ashamed that they were naked, and made clothes out of fig leaves to hide their bodies from each other and from God. They were also ashamed of what they had done, and hid from God when they heard Him walking in the garden. "Their love relationship with God, and each other, is permanently distorted...The man fears God; 'I was afraid.' The man runs from God; 'I was naked and hid myself.' The man blames God and the woman; 'The woman whom you gave to be with me, she gave me fruit from the tree, and I ate.'...Fear, flight, blame—the inevitable consequences of experiencing evil. Relationship with God is now jeopardized by humanity's choice of disobedience. Their choice doesn't expand their humanity, rather it is diminished...Evil sends waves of destruction crashing over all creation...Graciously acting to limit evil, God banishes the man and woman from the Garden of Eden ([Gen.] 3:21–24). Evil may be powerful, but it is neither all-pervasive nor eternal. God will set boundaries."[5]

Bryant Myers, in his book *Walking With the Poor*, says, "By now, the point of the story should be clear. From the day our first parents walked out of the garden, estranged from God, each other, and the earth itself, God has been at work redeeming...the fallen creation, its people, and its social systems. God's goal is to restore us...to our original identity and purpose, as children reflecting God's image, and to our original vocation as productive stewards, living together in just and peaceful relationships."[6]

In his famous book *When Bad Things Happen to Good People* (Schocken Books, 1981), author Rabbi Harold S. Kushner concludes that because bad things happen, God is either not all loving or not all powerful. I disagree with the good rabbi. In fact, the reason that bad things happen to good people is that we live in a fallen world riddled by sin. God, by His own design, gave man a free will, and we are still suffering from the consequences of Adam and Eve's fateful decision to disobey God and eat from the tree they were told not to eat from. The problem rests not with God, but with us.

There is, in fact, no one who is good:

- "Everyone has turned away, all have become corrupt; there is no one who does good, not even one" (Ps. 53:3, NIV).

- "There is no one righteous—no, not one" (Rom. 3:10).

There is no doubt that *ra* is all around us. Anyone who doesn't know that must be living like an ostrich with his head in the sand. Almost every day we hear of horrific attacks carried out by Islamic extremists, deadly earthquakes, tornadoes, hurricanes, floods, and other natural disasters—and they seem to be happening more often. *Ra* comes at us in the form of sickness, crime, accidents, and in many other ways. But God is constantly working to transform *ra* into *shalom*—especially for those who know and love Him. He holds us in the palm of His hand.

The Bible is filled with examples of how God has turned defeat into victory and delivered His people from evil and harm.

- For Daniel, *ra* took the form of hungry lions. But God shut the beasts' mouths and elevated Daniel to a position of great authority in the kingdom.

- *Ra* came for Shadrach, Meshach, and Abednego in the shape of a fiery furnace. But it was in that furnace that the three pious young men were joined by a fourth, the Son of God! (See Daniel 3:25.)

- Joseph faced the evil of his brothers' jealousy and the false accusations of Potiphar's wife but went on to become the second most powerful man in the entire world—saving millions of people from death by starvation, including his own family.

- And then, of course, there is Yeshua Himself, who underwent a brutal betrayal and torture followed by an agonizing crucifixion but rose victorious from the grave to defeat death and atone for the sins of mankind once and for all.

Keep this in mind as you face the inevitable trials and tribulations of life. Jesus never promised a life free from adversity to those who chose to follow Him. In fact, He promised that like Him, we would be ridiculed and persecuted for our faith. He told us we would endure hardship for the sake of the gospel. Yes, you will face crisis, disappointment, and some tragedy, just like every human being does. But remember as you face these challenges that God is the solution, not the problem. We live in a fallen world, and that reality affects us all. But turn to the Lord and He will help you navigate through it to victory. For "in all these things we are more than conquerors through Him who loved us" (Rom. 8:37).

So keep pressing on through the valleys of life and you will make it through. As the psalmist reminds us in Psalm 30:5, "Weeping may endure for a night, but joy comes in the morning" (MEV).

Chapter 7

GOD WILL GIVE YOU HOPE

*"For I know the plans I have for you," declares
the LORD, "plans to prosper you and not to harm
you, plans to give you hope and a future."*

—JEREMIAH 29:11, NIV, EMPHASIS ADDED

We wait in hope for the LORD; he is our help and our shield.

—PSALM 33:20, NIV

But now these three remain—faith, hope, and love.

—1 CORINTHIANS 13:13

THE TORAH CONTAINS more than one hundred names for God. Each of these names speaks of a different aspect of His character.

He is called *El-Shaddai*, or "God Almighty"; *Adonai*, which is translated as "Lord"; and *Yaweh-yireh*, "the God who provides." Other names include *Yaweh-rofeka*, "the God our healer," and *Yaweh-Tikvah*, which means "the Lord our hope."

In Acts 28:20, the Apostle Paul refers to Yeshua as "the hope of Israel." Of course, He is more than the hope of Israel; He is, in fact, the hope of the whole world. The futures of everyone and everything on this planet depend on Him.

Israel's national anthem is titled *HaTikvah*, "The Hope," and I think that's appropriate. The State of Israel is surrounded by enemies that desire her destruction. Many nations in the Middle East would like to see Israel disappear. Jews in Israel know what it's like to have to scramble to bomb shelters because another missile attack is underway. Bombs and rockets are a constant threat. It's extremely rare for a few days to go by without at least one missile launched against Israel.

And yet the Jewish people continue to have hope in God. They hold fast to King David's words in Psalm 23: "Even though I walk through the valley of the shadow of death, I will fear no evil, for You are with me: Your rod and Your staff comfort me. You prepare a table before me in the presence of my enemies. You have anointed my head with oil, my cup overflows" (vv. 4–5).

GOD GIVES US *TIKVAH*

The Hebrew word for hope is *tikvah* (תקוה). *Tikvah*, which is found in the Scriptures thirty-three times, means something expected, yearned for, or anticipated. It comes from the verb *kavah* (קוה), which can mean to stretch like a rope.

The first reference to *tikvah* is found in the Book of Judges, where Rahab hung a scarlet cord in her window to signify her faith in the God of Israel. You may remember the story: Joshua sent men to spy out the city of Jericho in preparation for an attack. Believing that God would deliver Jericho into the hands of the Israelites, Rahab took the spies into her house and hid them from the authorities. Then she told them:

> So now, please swear to me by ADONAI, since I have dealt kindly with you, that you also will deal kindly with my father's house. Give me a true sign that you will spare the lives of my father, my mother, my brothers, my sisters and all who belong to them, and save our lives from death.
>
> —JOSHUA 2:12–14

Then the men said to her:

> Tie this line of scarlet thread in the window through which you lowered us down, and gather to yourself in the house your father, your mother, your brothers and all your father's household—whoever goes out of the doors of your house into the street, his blood will be on his head and we will be innocent, but whoever is with you in the house, his blood will be on our head if any hand is laid on him.
>
> —JOSHUA 2:18–19

So she said:

> According to your words, so be it. Then she sent them away. After they had gone, she tied the scarlet cord to the window.
>
> —JOSHUA 2:21

As Rahab feared, God did deliver the city of Jericho into the hands of the Israelites. But because of the scarlet thread hanging in her window, she and her entire family were spared. *Tikvah* spares us from harm and gives us life.

The word *tikvah* is found twelve times in the Book of Job, expressing the fact that there is hope even in the midst of Job's seemingly hopeless situation. Perhaps the best definition of the word is "confident expectation." We are not talking about wishful thinking, as in, "Oh, I *wish* God would give me a good job or a beautiful wife or financial success. (You can fill in the blank.) I hope that's His will for me."

Tikvah is a firm assurance about things that are unseen and still in the future. It is based on the revealed Word of God and the voice of God's Spirit speaking to our hearts.

This kind of hope is so strong that it's like calling that which is not yet as though it already is. Abraham did this when he believed God's promise that he was going to father a son, even though he and Sarah were both advanced in years. This is what Joseph did when he told his family that he wanted them to take his bones out of Egypt and bury them in the Promised Land. It is what Moses showed as he led the children of Israel through the wilderness.

THE DIFFERENCE BETWEEN HOPE AND FAITH

Hope and faith, although very closely related, are different. Faith is in the present tense, "I believe *now*," while hope is expectation concerning the future, that which lies ahead. It's unswerving confidence that God will do what He said He will do at some future time.

Allow me to illustrate this idea. I have traveled so much internationally over the years that sometimes it seems that I've lived my life on airplanes. I'm always flying off somewhere—India, Ethiopia, Israel, and other countries all over the world. It's a rare thing when the airplane doesn't encounter some turbulence on one of these trips.

But there's turbulence—and then there's *turbulence*!

It's OK if the plane shakes a little bit, but on those rare occasions when you're somewhere over the middle of the Atlantic or the North Pole, the rivets and joints are squeaking and moaning, and the aircraft suddenly drops one hundred fifty or two hundred feet—now that's frightening!

You learn a lot about the people around you when you go through something like that. You can always spot the true Christians because they start praying. You can spot the charismatics because they are praying in tongues. Other people scream, start to cry, or fill the air with profanity, as if that's going to scare the plane and get it to start behaving. Yes, you see who people really are when they face something frightening like that. As the Bible says, those responses come straight out of the abundance of the heart. (See Matthew 12:34.)

In my case, such an experience always causes me to make sure I've repented of all sin, known and unknown, and I'm ready to face the Lord. In fact, I've been in one or two such situations over the years where I honestly didn't know if I was going to live or die. It really felt like the plane was going to break into pieces.

And then it always happens. Just when you're wondering if you're going to survive, the pilot comes on the loudspeaker and says in a calm voice: "Ladies and gentlemen, this is your pilot speaking. We're experiencing a little bit of turbulence right now, and we expect that the bumpy ride will continue for the next few minutes. But we're going to drop our altitude by about four thousand feet—and in another fifteen minutes or so we should be just fine. So keep your seat belts fastened, sit back, and enjoy the ride."

Here's what amazes me. As soon as the pilot makes that reassuring announcement, everything is better. The whole atmosphere of the plane changes. You can tangibly feel the tension and fear diminish. Believers shift from petition mode to a "thank You, Lord" mode. The charismatics shift from an intense, intercessory tongue to quietly singing melodic praises. People who were screaming and crying just moments earlier turn their attention back to their movies and magazines. And the ones who were so angry and profane are now ringing the flight attendants to order another drink. It is an amazing phenomenon. And it always happens the same way.

Now imagine what would happen if the pilot came on the public address system and in a frightened, shaky voice blurted out: "Ladies and gentlemen, I've never been through anything like this before. Can someone help? If there's anyone back there who thinks they can get us through this, please come to the cockpit right now. We need you!"

Just think of the panic that would ensue.

Thankfully, that's not likely to ever happen, because pilots are fully trained for those types of situations. They've been doing their job year in and year out. They've logged thousands of miles in the air. Turbulence is nothing for them. Plus, they have all the instruments and constant communication with air traffic controllers on the ground. They've been though this a hundred times, and they know the plane is built to handle it.

They know there's calm air at either a lower or higher altitude and that the turbulence is only temporary.

So when a pilot speaks with the calm voice of experience and authority, everybody on board relaxes. The airplane may still be shaking and rolling like crazy. It might even be worse than it was a few minutes ago, but because the pilot knows the outcome and he just said that everything is going to be all right, everyone relaxes and calms down.

LET GOD
TAKE CONTROL

God is the seasoned, expert pilot of your life. In fact, He is the perfect pilot. He knows how to get you safely through any storm life can throw at you. God is saying, "Yes, you will go through trials, tribulation, and painful experiences you may not understand, but in the midst of it all, I have a plan for you—and you will make it through. Just trust in Me." You will experience turbulence from time to time. But if you tune in to the Pilot, you'll hear a still, small voice of peace telling you that everything is going to be all right. That's the kind of hope God wants you to walk in.

As Jesus said, "In this world you will have trouble. But take heart! I have overcome the world" (John 16:33, NIV).

God not only wants to prosper you and keep you from harm, but He also wants to give you hope, confident expectation, and a future.

There is an old Jewish tale about a rabbi who became friends with a powerful king. The king enjoyed having the rabbi around because he was such a deep thinker, and because no difficulty ever seemed to trouble him or catch him off guard. He saw God's plan in everything that happened, something that amazed and amused the king, but also comforted him.

The two men often talked for hours about the deepest issues of life, and the king grew so fond of the rabbi that he wanted the fellow along with him wherever he went.

One day, the king took the rabbi into the forest to go hunting, even though the rabbi protested that he had never shot a gun and didn't really know anything about hunting. The rabbi was right to be worried. As they were deep in the forest, he stumbled and accidentally pulled his gun's trigger. The blast struck the king in the hand and blew away his little finger.

The king screamed in pain, as the rabbi ran to his side, apologizing profusely and trying to help the king's servants attend to the wound.

His apology did no good. The angry, hurting king ordered his men to throw the rabbi in a dungeon and leave him there for the rest of his life.

A year went by, and then another. And although the king missed the long talks with his former friend, every time he looked at his injured hand, anger rose up in him, and he was happy to know the rabbi was languishing in prison.

Then the king went on a hunting trip into one of the most primitive and dangerous regions of the jungle. Somehow, in the dark confusion of the rain forest, the king became separated from his hunting party.

The trees, shrubs, and tangled vines were so thick, he could not see more than a few feet in front of him. Suddenly he found himself surrounded by a band of cannibals wielding long, deadly looking spears. It was almost as if they had suddenly appeared out of thin air. They tied his hands behind him and marched him off to their village, jabbing at him with their spears to ensure that he didn't try to escape.

They babbled with excitement all the way, possibly about the good meal they were going to have later that evening.

But when they got back to their village, something strange happened.

One of the cannibals suddenly noticed the king's missing finger. He grabbed the injured hand and thrust it out where the others could see it. They all gathered around and engaged in what seemed to be a heated conversation about the missing finger.

After about ten or fifteen minutes of this, the cannibals untied the king, pointed into the jungle, and shouted at him. Apparently they wanted him to go, and he didn't have to be told twice. Stumbling as he ran, he headed as fast as he could back toward the spot where he'd become separated from his group.

What had happened? The cannibals had decided that his missing finger made him unfit for consumption. There was something wrong with him, and they weren't going to take any chances. Eating him might bring bad luck. The hunting accident that had crippled him had also saved his life.

The king was reunited with his party, returned home to his kingdom, and—at his first opportunity—went to the prison and ordered that his old friend be released from the dungeon. When he saw the rabbi, he put his arms around him and, with tears running down his face, apologized for putting him in prison. He then told about his close encounter with the cannibals.

"Do you understand what I'm saying?" the king asked. "When you shot my hand, you saved my life—and I put you in prison for it."

The rabbi just smiled. "It was all part of God's plan."

"How can you say that God wanted you to spend two years of your life in prison?" the king asked.

"Simple," came the answer. "If I was not in prison, I would have been with you in the jungle."

"Yes?"

"Yes. And there's nothing wrong with my hand. Those cannibals would have let you go—but they would have eaten me. God put me in prison to save *my* life."

As I said, that's an old story, and as far as I know, it has absolutely no basis in fact. But it does make the point that if we trust God, even when we don't understand the "whys," we can be sure that He always has our best interest at heart. Things that may seem bad when they happen to us may actually turn out for good because they are part of His divine plan for our lives.

No matter what may be going on in the world around you, you can always have hope. God is in charge, He knows what He's doing, and He knows the beginning from the end. As a child of God, I can assure you of this: He has a happy ending planned for you.

We can always experience hope, regardless of the situation, when we meditate on this truth found in Romans chapter 8, verses 17–18 (NIV):

> Now if we are children, then we are heirs—heirs of God and co-heirs with [Messiah], if indeed we share in his sufferings in order that we may also share in his glory. I consider that our present sufferings are not worth comparing with the glory that will be revealed in us.

Jesus Himself promises that our future is secure with Him. Be encouraged with these words of hope:

> Do not let your hearts be troubled. You believe in God; believe also in me. My Father's house has many rooms; if that were not so, would I have told you that I am going there to prepare a place for you? And if I go and prepare a place for you, I will come back and take you to be with me that you also may be where I am.
>
> —JOHN 14:1–3, NIV

Chapter 8

GOD WILL GIVE YOU A GLORIOUS FUTURE

*"For I know the plans I have for you," declares
the LORD, "plans to prosper you and not to harm
you, plans to give you hope and a future."*

—JEREMIAH 29:11, NIV, EMPHASIS ADDED

Your beginnings will seem humble, so prosperous will your future be.

—JOB 8:7, NIV

*Know also that wisdom is like honey for you: If you find it, there
is a future hope for you, and your hope will not be cut off.*

—PROVERBS 24:14, NIV

I T IS REPORTED that over three hundred years ago, King Louis XIV of France asked Blaise Pascal, the great Christian philosopher, to give him proof of the existence of God. Pascal replied, "Why the Jews, your Majesty, the Jews!"[1] What Pascal meant was that according to all logic, the Jewish people should have faded into history long ago, along with all the other nations we read about in the pages of the Torah.

The Amalekites are gone. So are the Philistines, the Ishmaelites, Jebusites, and all the other "ites." The Babylonians and the Assyrians, once two of the greatest, most powerful nations on earth, disappeared long ago. Only the Jews remain.

In his book *The Message in the Bottle* Walker Percy writes:

> Why does no one find it remarkable that in most world cities today there are Jews but not one single Hittite, even though the Hittites had a great flourishing civilization while the Jews nearby were a weak and obscure people?
>
> When one meets a Jew in New York or New Orleans or Paris or Melbourne, it is remarkable that no one considers the event remarkable...if there are Jews here, why are there not Hittites here?...Show me one Hittite in New York City.[2]

Calvin Miller says:

> "Where are the Hittites?" is a fair question. It has no clear answer. Perhaps the Hittites are no longer around because they failed to answer God's call. How we must cherish our call, our partnership with God. To lose this, or never to know it, is to lose our identity. To lose our call is never to matter to God. It is to die unused—to go wherever the Hittites went.
>
> But how do we keep from walking the Hittite edges

of our own irrelevancy? We are his people, his servants—
born to hurt and to cling to our call. Yet we are not just
born to cling; we are born to celebrate our calling. We
are the God-called who accept our hurt and bless our
brokenness.[3]

What makes the history of the Jews even more surprising is
that the Jews have survived and thrived, despite many attempts
to destroy them. The ancient pharaoh tried to destroy the
Israelites by killing all the male infants. The twelve tribes of
Israel were carried into captivity by the Assyrians and later the
Babylonians. Jerusalem was again destroyed by the Romans in
the first century and the Jews forced into the Diaspora. The
Crusaders, marching through Europe on their quest for the
Holy Land during the early centuries of the Middle Ages,
slaughtered entire Jewish communities. During the Spanish
Inquisition at the end of the fifteenth and into the sixteenth
century, Jews were forced to convert to Christianity and then
banished from Spain and Portugal. Countless thousands of
Jews were eventually put to death. Less than a century ago, the
Nazis exterminated over six million Jews along with millions of
other "undesirables" such as gypsies, the elderly, and the infirm,
in their attempt to wipe the Jews off the face of the earth. It
would take pages to list all of the other attempts that have been
made to eradicate the Jews. In my book *A Rabbi Looks at the
Last Days*, I wrote about some of the more recent ones:[4]

The Suez War of 1956: In the early 1950s, Egypt closed the
Suez Canal to Israeli ships. The United Nations ordered the
canal open, but Egypt refused. Then, Egypt's President Nasser
sent scores of terrorists into Israel, saying, "Egypt has decided
to dispatch her heroes, the disciples of Pharaoh and the sons of
Islam and they will cleanse the land of Palestine...There will

be no peace on Israel's border because we demand vengeance, and vengeance is Israel's death."

His foreign minister, Muhammad Salah al-Din, added, "We shall not be satisfied except by the final obliteration of Israel from the map of the Middle East."

After hundreds of Israelis were killed, Israel had no choice but to retaliate. The Egyptian army was quickly and easily defeated, and Israeli troops pushed deep into Egyptian territory before a cease-fire was declared. President Eisenhower pressured the Israeli government to return the land that had been conquered in battle, and Israel complied and returned the Sinai Peninsula

The Six-Day War of 1967: On May 20, 1967, Syria's Defense Minister Hafez al-Assad announced, "Our forces are now entirely ready to…explode the Zionist presence in the Arab homeland. The Syrian army, with its finger on the trigger, is united…I, as a military man, believe that the time has come to enter into a battle of annihilation."

Ten days later, Israel's old enemy, President Nasser of Egypt, said, "The armies of Egypt, Jordan, Syria, and Lebanon are poised on the borders of Israel…while standing behind us are the armies of Iraq, Algeria, Kuwait, Sudan, and the whole Arab nation. This act will astound the world. Today they will know that the Arabs are arranged for battle, the critical hour has arrived. We have reached the stage of serious action and not declarations."

The world was astounded, all right. After six days of war, the Arab coalition was utterly defeated.

The Yom Kippur War of 1973: The next war began on October 6, 1973. It was Yom Kippur, the holiest day in the Jewish calendar. Israel did not expect and was not prepared for the coordinated surprise attack undertaken by Egypt and

Syria. On the Golan Heights, fewer than 200 Israeli tanks faced an invasion of 1,400 tanks from Syria. Along the Suez Canal, some 436 Israeli soldiers tried to hold off an estimated 80,000 Egyptian troops.

At least nine Arab countries were actively engaged in the assault on Israel, contributing troops, weapons, and/or money. Libya's Muammar Gaddafi sent $1 billion in military aid to Egypt...

This has been life for the people of Israel. They are either at war, or being threatened by war.

Again, there is no way, other than God's intervention, that the Israeli people could have withstood the constant attacks against them.

Today Jews in many parts of the world continue to face ongoing persecution and violence. And yet the physical descendants of Abraham, Isaac, and Jacob continue to grow in economic strength and numbers. Why? There's only one reasonable explanation, and it is a supernatural one. God has protected and guarded the Jewish people. He promised to watch over them and give them a future, and He has done so.

In Jeremiah 29:11 He promised in the midst of their exile to give them a future...and by application, the same promise applies to us, those who "love God and are called according to His purpose." This promise is for you, today.

ACHARIT IS THE HEBREW WORD FOR FUTURE

Out of all the Hebrew words I've talked about from the promise God gives us in Jeremiah 29:11, I think this is my favorite word of all. *Acharit* (אחרית) literally means "to have an expected end." But it's more than that. It suggests that everything that is behind us, or all that we have left behind or gone through in our past, is part of a journey to a specific outcome. It carries the idea of an already settled destination; a preplanned destiny for our lives.

It reminds me of the old country preacher who held up his Bible and said, "Brothers and sisters, you may have trouble in this world. But I've looked in the back of this Book, and I know the way it's all going to turn out. In the end, we win!"

During their time of captivity in Babylon, God spoke to the exiled Jews through the prophet Jeremiah:

> "Again I will build you, so you will be rebuilt, virgin Israel! Again you will take up your tambourines as ornaments, and go out to dances of merrymakers. Again you will plant vineyards on the hills of Samaria—planters will plant and use them…Behold, I will bring them from the north country, and I will gather them from the ends of the earth—among them the blind and the lame, the pregnant together with she who is in labor with child. A great throng will return here. With weeping and supplications they will come. I will bring them, leading them to walk by streams of water on a straight path where they will not stumble. For I am Israel's father, and Ephraim is My first-born." Hear the word of ADONAI, O nations, and declare it in the distant islands, and say: "He who scattered Israel will gather and watch over him, as a shepherd does his flock."
>
> —JEREMIAH 31:3–4, 7–9

MARK TWAIN ON THE JEWS

The Scriptures contain many more of God's promises to the Jewish people. He promised to give His chosen people a future, and He has. In 1899 Mark Twain wrote an article about the Jewish people for *Harper's Magazine*. He said:

> If statistics are right, the Jews constitute but one per-
> cent of the human race. It suggests a nebulous dim puff
> of star dust lost in the blaze of the Milky Way. Properly
> the Jew ought hardly to be heard of, but he...is as promi-
> nent on the planet as any other people, and his commer-
> cial importance is extravagantly out of proportion to the
> smallness of his bulk. His contributions to the world's list
> of great names in literature, science, art, music, finance,
> medicine, and abstruse learning are also way out of pro-
> portion to the weakness of his numbers. He has made a
> marvelous fight in the world, in all the ages; and has done
> it with his hands tied behind him...
>
> The Egyptian, the Babylonian, and the Persian rose,
> filled the planet with sound and splendor, then faded to
> dream-stuff and passed away; the Greek and the Roman
> followed...other peoples have sprung up and held their
> torch high for a time, but it burned out, and they sit in
> twilight now, or have vanished. The Jew saw them all,
> beat them all, and is now what he always was, exhibiting
> no decadence, no infirmities of age, no weakening of his
> parts, no slowing of his energies, no dulling of his alert
> and aggressive mind. [5]

TOLSTOY ON THE JEWS

Russian novelist Leo Tolstoy shared Twain's view of the Jewish people:

> What is the Jew?...What kind of unique creature is this
> whom all the rulers of all the nations of the world have
> disgraced and crushed and expelled and destroyed; perse-
> cuted, burned and drowned; and who, despite their anger

and their fury, continues to live and to flourish. What is this Jew whom they have never succeeded in enticing with all the enticements in the world, whose oppressors and persecutors only suggested that he deny (and disown) his religion and cast aside the faithfulness of his ancestors?! The Jew—is the symbol of eternity....He is the one who for so long had guarded the prophetic message and transmitted it to all humankind. A people such as this can never disappear. The Jew is eternal. He is the embodiment of eternity. [6]

The same God who has supernaturally preserved the Jewish people and brought them back from captivity to their own land in fulfillment of His word will fulfill every promise He has made to you in His Word.

GOD WILL DIRECT YOUR DECISIONS

One of my favorite scriptures in the Bible is Proverbs 3:5–6. It says, "Trust in the LORD with all your heart, and lean not on your own understanding; in all your ways acknowledge Him, *and He shall direct your paths*" (NKJV, emphasis added).

As long as we endeavor to obey His Word and spend time with Him, He will guide and direct our lives. God works in sovereign and sometimes mysterious ways to move us toward the future He has preordained for us.

We see this truth declared clearly in many other scriptures. Another one I love is, "The steps of a good man are ordered by the LORD, and He delights in his way" (Ps. 37:23, NKJV).

In a given week, we have to make dozens of decisions. As believers, we're constantly faced with the question, "Do I go left here, or do I turn right?" Some of the decisions we face are difficult to make. How do we navigate, knowing that many of the decisions we make today will have an outcome later on, either for good or not-so-good? Do we buy or rent a home? How do we invest our retirement? Should I trust this person? When do I say yes and when do I say no? Decisions, decisions, decisions. Some of us *hate* making them because we know our decisions have consequences. Some are minor, others have a huge impact on us and those around us.

Most of us have seen homeless people on the streets of our communities. Ragged men and women stand at intersections, holding up signs that say something like, "Hungry! Please help."

In our inner cities, there are people who live in cardboard boxes and survive by eating scraps of food fished out of dumpsters. Some have just fallen on bad times, but many are alcoholics or addicts. How did they get there? There is no way they decided early in life, "When I grow up I want to be the best homeless alcoholic or drug addict I can be. I'm going to study hard, do a four-year program, maybe get a graduate degree, and then I'm going to become a drunkard, druggie, or homeless mendicant."

That's not what happened.

Somewhere in the past—perhaps a year, a decade, or even thirty years ago—that person took his first drink or first illicit drug. He didn't realize then that the *acharit* at the end of that decision would leave him sitting on the side of the road begging for money for his next bottle of booze or bag of heroin. If he had known where that first step was going to lead him, he never would have taken it.

I've been told that there is a small spring in the Rocky Mountains that produces two streams of water. One heads west and the other east. Each of them joins larger bodies of water as it rolls along. The stream that flows eastward eventually becomes part of the Mississippi River and goes on to the Gulf of Mexico, which is part of the Atlantic Ocean. The other stream eventually reaches the Gulf of California and becomes part of the Pacific Ocean. They start at the same place, but a "decision" on which way to turn eventually leaves them an entire continent apart. The decisions we make are this important.

Acharit not only means "an expected end," it also means "that which is behind." In other words, it's about connecting the dots of our past decisions to understand how we got to where we are today.

Here's a good example. If you spend more than you make, you will eventually go into debt. You can pray and confess the scriptures "my God shall supply for all of my needs" and "He will do exceedingly, abundantly more than I can ask or think" until you're blue in the face, but you will still sink deeper and deeper into debt if you aren't following the principles of good stewardship and you continue overspending.

Foolish decisions will result in bad outcomes. Wise decisions will result in good outcomes. It is not just about prayer and walking in faith; we also have to apply God's wisdom. We need to obey the principles found in His Word and follow wise council.

Maybe you have made some foolish decisions and you are living with the consequences of those decisions. I have some good news for you. God is gracious, forgiving, and longsuffering, and He will help you turn things around. You may have to make some major changes, but if you repent and you are willing to change, He will give you the power to make those necessary changes. Sometimes your situation will improve immediately, even supernaturally. In other cases it may take some time and some work. Just hang in there, press on, and don't give up!

Even the alcoholic or drug addict living on the street can experience the transforming power of God and be set on a new course. It happens every day, because God is a miracle-working, life-transforming God.

It is never too late. I am sure you've heard the adage, "Today is the first day of the rest of your life." Well, it's true. So don't put off those things you need to change any longer.

GUIDANCE FROM ABOVE

One of the greatest technological advances in our lifetime (there are so many it is mind boggling) is the Global Positioning System or GPS. I am not sure exactly how it all works since it is so complex, but it is very easy to use. You simply enter your intended destination, and a very sweet, patient voice tells you what roads to take, where and when to turn, how far you have to go, and how long it will take you to get there. If you miss your exit or make a wrong turn, the voice will tell you to make a U-turn, or the GPS will re-plot a new route almost instantly.

Before we had this, I used to get lost regularly. Even though my wife would implore me to stop and ask for directions, I would ignore her until she would finally yell at me and I would give in. (I know I am not the only male out there who refuses to ask for directions!) But now we have GPS and we don't have to get lost anymore!

Just think of it. Satellites way above the earth's atmosphere are able to triangulate our position and determine the best route to get us from point A to point B. We don't know how to get where we want to go, we can't see from up above, but with GPS we just plug in our intended destination (I even do it with voice commands now) and away we go! Some apps even factor in the traffic, road construction, and any accidents, and will reroute you based on this information. It is amazing.

In the same way, we live our lives in a finite realm. We can't see what will happen in the future or know the outcome of our decisions. If we did, we would all be rich because we would know what stocks to buy or exactly when to buy or sell our homes or other investments. Wouldn't that be nice?

But God, who "sits above the circle of the earth" (Isa. 40:22), *does* know everything. He knows the outcome of every decision. He knows the future. He knows every need we have—before we even have the need. Every hair on your head is numbered. He is infinite and lives above the timeline of our daily lives.

As Isaiah 46:10 tells us, God sees the end from the beginning. In the same way a GPS application can guide and direct us to our destination through satellites orbiting far above the surface of the earth, God, who "dwells above and sees all," can guide us to our *acharit*, our expected end. He is able and, perhaps more importantly, He is willing to guide us on a day-by-day basis to make the right decisions so we can prosper and avoid the pitfalls and evils (*ra*) of wrong decisions.

But you have to do your part. You have to spend enough time in His presence and in His Word to hear and recognize His voice. You have to live by the principles found in the Scriptures. You need to ask, "God, what will the outcome be if I go this way? Where will this decision ultimately bring me?" Because He is infinite, He can show you the *acharit* of the path you are taking.

When I read Jeremiah 29:11, I believe God is saying, "My plan for you includes giving you the supernatural ability to make the right decisions and know what the result of those decisions will be. How? By coming up with Me and seeing how things look from My point of view." Wow! What a promise! God's plan for you allows you to access His wisdom to make choices and decision. As James says, "If any of you lacks wisdom, let him ask of God, who gives to all without hesitation and without fault, and it will be given to him" (James 1:5).

God does more than offer you an opportunity to wind up in a good place. He gives you the confidence of knowing that He is working and leading your life. As Hebrews 12:2 says, He is "the initiator and perfecter of faith."

God is absolutely committed to you. He has a destiny for your life, and He has given you the talents and abilities you need to achieve it. Through His power working in and through you, you'll be able to fulfill that destiny He ordained for you before you were even born. And when you reach that expected end and take your last breath, you will experience the joy of facing Jesus eye-to-eye and hearing Him say, "Well done, good and faithful servant! You were faithful with a little, so I'll put you in charge of much. Enter into your master's joy!" (Matt. 25:23).

GOD'S AMAZING LOVE

Do you understand how much God loves you?

Ken Gaub was a member of a Christian family musical group that traveled the country performing concerts and telling people about the love of God.[7]

At first he had a great passion for what he was doing. He put his heart into every song, and he really meant it when he talked about the joy and new life found through a relationship with Jesus.

But as time went by, the passion faded. He sang the same songs so many times that they began to lose their meaning. He gave the same messages, the same answers to people's questions.

He was going through the motions, and even began to wonder if God was really involved in what he and his family were doing. He spent a lot of time telling people how to have a relationship with God, and yet his own relationship with his heavenly Father was badly in need of repair. "We travel around so much, I don't know if even God knows where we are," he said.

Gaub was considering quitting the musical group and getting a regular job. He didn't exactly know what he wanted to do, but it would be good to stay in one place instead of traveling from town to town on a bus.

He was thinking about all of these things when the family bus stopped in a small town in Ohio on the way to another concert. Everyone else, including his wife, got off the bus and walked into town to get some lunch. But Ken decided to stay behind to think and pray about whether or not he should do something else with his life.

After a while, he began to feel thirsty. He saw a gas station a block or so away and decided to walk there and get a soda. He hadn't gone too far when he began to hear the shrill sound of a ringing telephone. He looked around and saw an empty phone booth a bit farther down the street. His first impulse was to walk on past. There was no one else around, so it obviously must be a wrong number. But when the phone kept ringing, his curiosity got the best of him.

He stepped into the booth, picked up the phone, and spoke into the receiver.

"Hello?"

"Person-to-person call for Ken Gaub," an operator said.

His heart began pounding.

"You're crazy!" he said. "That's impossible."

For a moment he thought he must be on one of those hidden-camera TV shows. He spun around in the booth, looking for the camera, but didn't find one.

Then another voice came on the line. "I believe that's him. I believe that's him."

"Well," the operator asked, "is Ken Gaub there?"

He cleared his throat. "Yes, I'm Ken Gaub."[8]

Gaub found himself connected to a woman who had been planning to commit suicide. Her life was a mess, and she just didn't think she could take it anymore. She was about to end it all, when she remembered watching a television show and hearing a man named Ken Gaub talk about the love of Jesus. He seemed to be looking right at her, and his words were so comforting and sincere. If only she could talk to him, he might be able to give her some reason why she should go on living. Suddenly, in her mind's eyes, she saw a long string of numbers. She felt certain that God was telling her how to reach Ken Gaub by telephone. And she was right. She had even made the call person-to-person to ensure that she would be able to talk to Gaub himself.

It didn't take long for Ken Gaub to convince his caller that God loved her, had a plan for her life, and definitely did not want her to take her own life. Over the next several months, Gaub and his wife stayed in touch with the woman, counseling her and teaching her more about God's love, until they finally knew that her suicidal thoughts were behind her and she was strong enough to go on.

As for Ken Gaub, he rediscovered the passion he had lost somewhere along the way. He found that the message he was delivering really was powerful and had the ability to change lives forever. He also knew that his heavenly Father loved him dearly and always knew exactly where he was—even when he had spent so many hours on the bus that he himself didn't know![9]

Be encouraged today. God has a plan for your life, an expected end—an *acharit*. And He is committed to getting you there, for He is both the author and the finisher of your faith, and He will complete the good work that He has begun.

Chapter 9

SEEK FIRST HIS KINGDOM

But seek first the kingdom of God and His righteousness,
and all these things shall be added to you.

—MATTHEW 6:33

GOD IS NOT obligated to help people who never give Him a second thought.

Over my years in ministry, I have met a lot of people who were mad at God because He didn't help them out of some jam, bless a business venture, or intervene in some other way.

"Well, how much of your time do you devote to God?" I'll ask.

"Devote to God? I'm not sure what you mean."

"Do you go to a Bible study, church, or congregation?"

"No, I don't believe we need to do that."

"Do you read the Bible?"

"Uh, no, not really."

"How about prayer. Do you pray?"

"No, I'm not much of a pray-er. Well, I say a prayer before meals."

"Do you tithe?"

"Well, no, I don't believe in that. That's part of the law, and the law has been done away with."

Here's a nice Jewish word for you: *chutzpah*. It's pronounced "hutz' puh," and it might be translated as "nerve" or "audacity." I think it takes a lot of chutzpah to think that God is obligated to bless you, rescue you, and guide your decisions when you've never given Him as much as the time of day. So many treat God like a spare tire. He remains in the trunk until needed.

That is a misunderstanding of who God is. He is Almighty God, the Creator of the universe. We were created to serve Him, not the other way around.

Yes, God delights in giving you the desires of your heart, and as I've been explaining in this book, He certainly has a good plan and destiny for your life. But He also expects you to give Him and His kingdom the highest priority in your life.

GOD RUSHES TO THE RESCUE

Now, it is true that many people have come to believe in God or rededicated their lives to Yeshua after they called out to Him at some crisis point in their lives and He responded. I know a lot of people who have had experiences like that. Some weren't even sure God existed, but they cried out, "God, if You're there, please help me," and He showed up to rescue them. But once these people discovered that God was real, they began seeking a relationship with Him. They didn't think they could go on ignoring Him and expect that He would still come running anytime they called.

I'm not saying He wouldn't do that. His grace and mercy is limitless. Every time I read through the *Tenach* (the Old Testament) I'm amazed how often He forgave and continued to bless my forefathers despite their continual idolatry and wickedness. He never abandoned them, even when they reaped the consequences of their sin and rebellion and were sent into exile. He never stopped loving them and preserved them as a nation, eventually bringing them back to the land He promised through Abraham.

Ironically, it was during their captivity in Babylon that the Jewish people learned to put God first and cling to their faith. After seventy years away from their homeland, they were still yearning for home, still keeping the laws God had given them.

It was in Babylon that they discovered God's grace and willingness to forgive and forget. Our heavenly Father assures us that He is the One who blots out our transgressions and remembers our sins no more (Isa. 43:25).

In his book *The Ragamuffin Gospel*, Brennan Manning tells a story about a woman who began telling her friends and neighbors that she was having periodic visits from Jesus Himself:

The reports reached the archbishop...He decided to check her out. There is always a fine line between the authentic mystic and the lunatic fringe.

"Is it true, ma'am, that you have visions of Jesus?" asked the cleric.

"Yes," the woman replied simply.

"Well, the next time you have a vision, I want you to ask Jesus to tell you the sins that I confessed in my last confession."

The woman was stunned. "Did I hear you right, bishop? You actually want me to ask Jesus to tell me the sins of your past?"

"Exactly. Please call me if anything happens."

Ten days later the woman notified her spiritual leader of a recent apparition. "Please come," she said.

Within the hour the archbishop arrived. He trusted eye-to-eye contact. "You just told me on the telephone that you actually had a vision of Jesus. Did you do what I asked?"

"Yes, bishop, I asked Jesus to tell me the sins you confessed in your last confession."

The bishop leaned forward with anticipation. His eyes narrowed.

"What did Jesus say?"

She took his hand and gazed deep into his eyes. "Bishop," she said, "these are His exact words: *'I can't remember.'*"[1]

That's the way God is. When He forgives, He forgets. As He declared in the promise of the new covenant found in Jeremiah 31:31–34, He remembers our sins no more.

God is always willing to forgive and forget our sins as long as we repent and turn away from them. First John 1:9 says, "If we confess our sins, He is faithful and righteous to forgive our sins and purify us from all unrighteous." The problem is not that God won't forgive us, but that most of us have such a tough time forgiving ourselves. Carl Jung, the famous psychiatrist who founded analytical psychology, wrote about this in his book *Modern Man in Search of a Soul*:

> The acceptance of oneself is the essence of the whole moral problem and the epitome of a whole outlook upon life. That I feed the hungry, that I forgive an insult, that I love my enemy in the name of Christ [Messiah]—all these are undoubtedly great virtues. What I do unto the least of my brethren, that I do unto Christ. But what if I should discover that the least amongst them all, the poorest of the beggars, the most impudent of all the offenders, the very enemy himself—that these are within me, and that I myself stand in need of the aims of my own kindness— that I myself am the enemy who must be loved—what then? As a rule, the Christian's attitude is then reversed; there is no longer any question of love or long-suffering; we say to the brother within us "Raca," and condemn and rage against ourselves. We hide it from the world; we refuse to admit ever having met this least among the lowly in ourselves.[2]

Remember that Jesus said we are to love others as much as we love ourselves. From that, we can gather that He expects us to love ourselves. Self-love is not a sin or a crime unless it becomes an obsession.

Anyone who has ever taken a commercial flight is familiar with the safety talk the flight attendants give before the plane takes off. One of the things they tell you is that if there's a sudden decrease of air pressure in the cabin, oxygen masks will drop from the ceiling.

They also say that anyone traveling with small children should put their own mask on first and then help their children put on their masks.

That sounds counterintuitive. It seems logical that you'd help your child first and then—and only then—tend to your own needs. But it doesn't work that way. If you don't take care of your own need first, you might fall unconscious. And if that happened, you wouldn't be able to help yourself or your children. So often in life, we must love and care for ourselves before we can care properly for others.

You can be sure that God loves you more than anyone else has ever loved you. He loves you so much that He was willing to suffer and die for you. He longs to spend time with you. The Bible even says that He is jealous. (See Exodus 34:14, for example.) So again, the first reason you should spend time with God is because He loves you and wants to have your company.

Do you understand how much God loves you? Do you believe it? Do you realize that if you were the only sinner who needed to be spared from the horrors of hell, Yeshua still would have died for you?

Henri Nouwen hit the mark when he wrote:

> Over the years, I have come to realize that the greatest trap in our life is not success, popularity, or power, but self-rejection. Success, popularity, and power can indeed present a great temptation, but their seductive quality often comes from the way they are part of the much larger temptation to self-rejection. When we have come to believe in the voices that call us worthless and unlovable, then success, popularity, and power are easily perceived as attractive solutions. The real trap, however, is self-rejection. As soon as someone accuses me or criticizes me, as soon as I am rejected, left alone, or abandoned, I find myself thinking, "Well that proves once again that I am a nobody"...I deserve to be pushed aside, forgotten, rejected, and abandoned. Self-rejection is the

greatest enemy of the spiritual life because it contradicts the sacred voice that calls us the "Beloved." Being the Beloved constitutes the core truth of our existence.[3]

I know I've said this numerous times already, but I can't over-stress how much value there is in spending time with God in prayer, learning to hear His still, small voice, and reading His Word, the Bible, on a daily basis.

SEEK GOD DILIGENTLY

The next three verses that follow Jeremiah 29:11 read:

> "Then you will call on Me, and come and pray to Me, and I will listen to you. You will seek Me and find Me, when you will search for Me with all your heart. Then I will be found by you," says ADONAI, "and I will return you from exile, and gather you from all the nations and from all the places where I have driven you," says ADONAI, "and I will bring you back to the place from which I removed you as captives into exile."
> —JEREMIAH 29:12–14

While God's love is unconditional, His blessings are not. You and I have a part to play.

In order to receive the blessings that God has planned for you, you must put Him and His kingdom first in your life, and as the above Scripture says, search for Him with your whole heart. God has much to say about those who don't really care about having a relationship with Him:

> Since these people draw near with their mouths and honor Me with their lips, yet their hearts are far from Me...the

wisdom of their wise will perish, and the discernment of
their discerning will be concealed.

—ISAIAH 29:13–14

They have neither obeyed My voice nor walked according
to it, but have walked after the stubbornness of their
heart...Therefore...I will make this people eat worm-
wood and drink poisoned water. I will scatter them
among the nations whom neither they nor their fathers
have known. I will pursue them with the sword, until I
have finished with them.

—JEREMIAH 9:12–15

HOW TO SEEK GOD

What does it mean to seek God with your whole heart? How
can you be sure that you're right in step with Him, not running
ahead of Him or lagging behind?

How do you seek God diligently? I believe you seek Him
through prayer, meditation, studying the Scriptures, worship,
and actively seeking His guidance in every situation. I also
believe it means putting Him first in your life, no matter the cost.

When the Pharisees asked Jesus which commandment was
the greatest of all, He didn't hesitate: "You shall love ADONAI
your God with all your heart, and with all your soul, and with
all your strength, and with all your mind" (Luke 10:27).

God expects to be first in your life. That is because He knows
that you can only have the satisfactory, fulfilled life He wants
you to have if you put Him first.

- Ecclesiastes tells us that man was put on this
  earth to serve God. "Now all has been heard; here
  is the conclusion of the matter: Fear God and

keep his commandments, for this is the duty of
all mankind" (Eccles. 12:13, NIV).

- James says, "Draw near to God, and He will draw
  near to you" (James 4:8).

- Hebrews 11:6 says, "Now without faith it is impossible to please God. For the one who comes to
  God must believe that He exists and that He is a
  rewarder of those who seek Him."

I have an acquaintance who was born into a high-caste
Hindu family in India. His parents were extremely well-to-do,
and my friend was due to inherit their fortune.

His family did everything within their power to avoid even
associating with the lower castes. He remembers how his
mother went through their house every week on "trash day,"
sprinkling holy water to cleanse the place after servants from
lower castes had come to collect their garbage. According to
their belief in karma, this was one of the ways they protected
themselves from the sin and corruption. (Karma is the exact
opposite of grace, by the way. Karma says that we always suffer
from our sins. Grace says that Jesus took our sins upon Himself
when He atoned for our sins and we are set free from the
consequences.)

Things changed for my friend when, in his teens, someone
gave him a copy of the Gospel of John. He was deeply moved
when he read that God had sent His only Son to earth to give
His life as an atonement for our sins. Through the conviction of the Holy Spirit, he knew that what he was reading was
absolutely true and that He needed forgiveness for his sins. He
sought out a Christian pastor and prayed with him to receive
Jesus as His Lord and Savior.

He thought there would be serious consequences, and he was right. His parents didn't take the news well. In fact, they were furious. When they heard what he had done, they gave him an ultimatum: he would renounce what he had done, or else they would disown him. That meant they would cut him off without a penny to his name. They would no longer acknowledge that he was their son.

What would you do if you had been in his shoes? Most of us have never had to make such a difficult decision—especially those of us who have grown up in the United States. The Pilgrims came here seeking freedom to worship God in the way that seemed best to them, and most Americans still retain that freedom.

My friend didn't hesitate. It broke his heart to be cut off by his family, but he could not turn his back on his Savior. He chose Jesus, even though it meant the loss of his family, his fortune, and his standing in his community. It was like he was losing his own culture, everything he had grown up believing himself to be. But as the missionary martyr Jim Elliot said, "He is no fool who gives what he cannot keep to gain that which he cannot lose."[4]

For the last thirty years, my friend has faithfully and joyfully served God. He continues to serve the Lord diligently and has never given a thought to returning to his old way of life.

JEWISH LIKE JESUS

I can completely relate to the rejection my friend had to endure when his family cut him off and he was rejected by his community. Although the reaction of my family was not quite as severe, many of my Messianic Jewish brethren were completely cut off by their families and friends when they made the decision to follow Yeshua. In some cases, their parents actually sat *Shiva* (the act of mourning after a loved one dies and is buried) for them after declaring them dead!

In my case, my parents were very upset with me when I told them I had accepted Jesus as my Messiah. They felt betrayed. Although my father passed away a short time later, my faith estranged me from my mother for many years.

As I shared in my book *A Rabbi Looks at Jesus of Nazareth*[5], I was raised in a Reform Jewish home. My family always went to temple for the High Holy Days, and we celebrated Passover, Hanukkah, and the other significant Jewish feasts. I attended Hebrew school on Tuesdays and Thursdays and religious studies in Jewish history, culture, and tradition on Sundays. When I turned thirteen, I had my bar mitzvah, the rite of passage into adulthood for young Jewish males. But all of this had more to do with my Jewish heritage than it did with any sort of relationship with God. I learned all the Bible stories found in the Torah and the prophets, but they didn't seem to have much meaning or relevance for my life. It was like learning about the Pilgrims in school. It all happened a long time ago, and it didn't have anything to do with now.

In high school I had a wrestling coach who talked often and openly about his faith in Jesus. He had a sense of destiny, a sense of purpose. He seemed to know who he was and what he was supposed to do with his life. I sort of envied him, I guess. But that was for him, not for me. I wanted to have fun. And after all, I was Jewish—and Jews don't believe in Jesus.

Then, when I was an undergraduate business major at the University of Buffalo, a friend I hung out with and did drugs with got saved. I lost contact with her for a while, but when we reconnected, she began to witness to me. She shared with me how Jesus had brought her back from the brink of ruin and death. Actually, I had watched her slowly destroying herself by a growing addiction to drugs. She quit going to class. She lost weight. She quit caring about her appearance. After a while, I didn't see her at all. I felt bad about what had happened to her, but it wasn't really any of my business. I had my life, and she had hers.

Weeks went by, and then I ran into her one day. Everything about her had changed. She looked healthy. The sparkle was back in her eyes.

She explained to me that at the lowest point in her life, she walked into a pool hall and the owner, who had recently been saved, urged her to turn to Jesus. She had nothing to lose. She prayed with him and called out to God for help. He answered her prayer. In that moment, she was instantly delivered from drugs and set free.

Her story amazed me because I could see with my own eyes that something truly had happened to her. I was happy for her, but she needed a crutch—I didn't. I was happy with my life...so I thought.

After that, she called me constantly, telling me that God loved me and had a plan for my life. I didn't want to hear it, so I tried to keep my distance. But over time she wore me down, and I eventually agreed to go with her to her Bible study.

From the moment I walked into that room, I wanted to turn around and run. I felt totally out of place. Everyone was so strange...they just kept staring at me and smiling. It was eerie.

I wanted to leave, but for some reason, I couldn't.

After the study, the teacher and host invited me to join him upstairs in his living room. He placed a Bible in my lap and began to show me scriptures about sin and forgiveness.

As he shared, something strange began to happen. I don't know what else to call it except a supernatural experience. I didn't have a vision or hear a heavenly voice, but I was instantly and completely aware of my physical separation from God. The room became abnormally bright and warm. I began to sweat profusely, and I can honestly say that I felt as though that couch where I was sitting had arms that reached out and grabbed me—holding me in place.

It was so significant that the thought wandered through my head that perhaps the room had been rigged in such a way as to produce this amazing response! I even went back later to check out that couch and the lighting in the room, but found nothing irregular about either.

I had begun to deal with a sense of my own separation from a God who loved me. It was that plain and simple. Looking back at this event that happened over thirty years ago, I am convinced that the presence of God came into that room that evening and apprehended me. God had a plan for my life that was different from my own, and He meant to make sure I would lay aside my plans and follow Him.

Sadly, my parents felt that I had turned my back on my Jewish heritage and didn't understand when I told them that I had really done exactly the opposite. I tried to explain that, in surrendering myself to the Messiah, I had embraced my Jewishness in a way I had never done before, but that seemed preposterous to them.

One of the first things they did was send me to the rabbi.

"Your grandfather would be rolling over in his grave if he knew you'd done this," he said. "He would do anything to stop you." He told me, "Just as Adolf Hitler tried to destroy us (the

Jewish people) physically, you're aiding and abetting the enemy by seeking to destroy us spiritually."

Of course, I was saddened by the rabbi's attack on the One who had already become such a dear friend to me and such an important part of my life. I tried to tell him that when I surrendered to Yeshua, I had discovered I could have an intimate friendship with the Creator of the universe. But he didn't want to hear it.

As of today, this friendship has endured for more than thirty-six years, and I know it will last for the rest of my life on earth—and beyond. Now I don't just know *about* Him. I know Him personally.

THE AMAZING STORY OF CORNELIUS

Wonderful things happen when we seek God diligently. The story of Cornelius the Centurion in the tenth chapter of Acts is a prime example. Because Cornelius was a diligent seeker of God, the Lord chose him and his family to be the first Gentiles (non-Jews) to come into the kingdom.

Cornelius was a Roman army officer in charge of one hundred soldiers. Scripture tells us that he and all his family were "devout and God fearing." That doesn't necessarily mean they were converts to Judaism. In all likelihood they were not.

The Roman Empire was flourishing during the first century. It stretched across much of the known world, and thousands of Roman soldiers were stationed in occupied Israel. Many of them—as many as 10 percent, according to some historians—came to believe in the God of Israel while living among the Jewish people.

They had grown up learning about the Roman gods, who were often capricious, petty, vindictive, and devious. Some had served in other parts of the empire where people believed in even more such gods.

But when they came to Israel, soldiers like Cornelius were impressed and moved by the people's faith in one God—the God who had created the heavens and the earth and who had given the Jewish people a great moral law. The Roman gods seemed like poorly drawn cartoons when compared with the God the Jews worshipped.

It's possible that Cornelius and his family attended synagogue or visited the outer courts of the temple in Jerusalem. Many Romans did. And the Bible says that Cornelius was generous to those in need and prayed to God regularly.

One afternoon, as Cornelius was praying, an angel appeared to him and said, "Your prayers and *tzedakah* [gifts to the poor] have gone up as a memorial offering before God. Now send men to Joppa and call for Simon, also named Peter" (Acts 10:4–5).

Cornelius did exactly as the angel said. He called two of his servants, and "a devout soldier," who was one of his attendants, told them what had happened and dispatched them to Joppa (also called Jaffa or Yaffo), which was a round-trip of roughly sixty miles that would take three full days.

If you are familiar with the story, you know that just as Cornelius's messengers were nearing Joppa, God gave Peter an amazing vision:

> He saw heaven opened and something like a large sheet being let down to earth by its four corners. It contained all kinds of four-footed animals, as well as reptiles and birds. Then a voice told him, "Get up, Peter. Kill and eat."
>
> "Surely not, Lord!" Peter replied. "I have never eaten anything impure or unclean."

> The voice spoke to him a second time, "Do not call any-
> thing impure that God has made clean."
>
> —ACTS 10:11–15

The same vision was repeated three times.

Imagine how shocked Peter must have been. The Law of Moses prohibited the eating of many of the creatures Peter saw in that vision. Devout Jews had avoided eating these types of animals for many generations. This was a true paradigm shift. What could this vision possibly mean?

The Bible says that while Peter was still thinking about the vision, the men sent by Cornelius arrived at the house where he was staying. The Holy Spirit spoke to Peter and told him that three men were waiting for him downstairs, and that he was to go with them.

After hearing why they had come, Peter and several other believers headed out on the road for Caesarea. When they got there, they found a house full of people waiting to hear what they had to say. Peter started by reminding them that Jewish law forbade Jews from visiting with Gentiles or entering into their homes. "Yet God has shown me that I should call no one unholy or unclean. So I came without objection when I was sent for" (Acts 10:28–29).

When Cornelius told Peter about his angelic visitation, Peter said something that changed the world: "I truly understand that God is not one to show favoritism, but in every nation the one who fears Him and does what is right is acceptable to Him" (vv. 34–35).

The doors to the kingdom were flung wide open.

What happened next was even more startling: As Peter preached to them about Yeshua, "the Holy Spirit came on all who heard the message. The circumcised believers who had come with Peter were astonished that the gift of the Holy Spirit had been poured out even on Gentiles. For they heard them speaking in tongues and praising God" (Acts 10:44–46, NIV).

Incredible things happen when we seek God diligently. Sometimes the whole world changes.

Chapter 10

LEARN TO SEE YOURSELF THROUGH GOD'S EYES

He does not see a man as man sees, for man looks at the outward appearance, but ADONAI looks into the heart.

—1 SAMUEL 16:7

ONE OF THE important keys to receiving God's blessing is to see yourself the way He sees you. And how does He see you? As more than a conqueror. As someone who is able to do great things for His kingdom. As His precious child.

If you belong to Yeshua, He doesn't see you as weak, sinful, or as a failure in any way, and He doesn't want you to see yourself that way either. When He looks at you, He sees that you are covered by the blood of His only begotten Son. He says, "You are strong, the word of God abides in you, and you have overcome the evil one" (1 John 2:14).

BE STRONG LIKE MOSES

Can you imagine what Pharaoh thought the first time he saw Moses again after four decades?

He was the king of an empire, the unchallenged leader of one of the most powerful nations on the earth. He lived in a huge palace, surrounded by slaves that responded to his every whim. He wore the finest clothes, owned great quantities of gold, silver, and jewels—and was even worshipped as a god by his subjects. His word was absolute.

Moses, on the other hand, had been tending sheep in the desert for forty years. Yes, it's true that, although he was a Jew, he had been born in Egypt, adopted by the king's daughter, and grown up in luxury. But those days were long forgotten. Moses was eighty years old when God sent him to free the Israelites. He had fled Egypt forty years earlier after killing an Egyptian who had been beating a Hebrew. There is no indication that anyone in Egypt remembered or recognized him.

He had left Egypt as a member of the royal family, but he returned as an ordinary shepherd. His face and hands were undoubtedly weathered by years spent tending the flocks of his father-in-law, Jethro, in the deserts of Midian. Here he was, showing up in Pharaoh's palace, claiming he was a messenger from the one true God, and that he had come on behalf of the Hebrew people.

Pharaoh must have been tempted to laugh out loud. How could a mere shepherd have the nerve to appear before such a mighty king, much less make demands of him? Why, this poor fellow must have spent too much time in the hot sun. Clearly, it had affected his brain.

Moses himself had tried to convince God to choose someone else when the Lord first spoke to him from a burning bush and called him to lead the children of Israel out of captivity in Egypt. "Who am I, that I should go to Pharaoh, and bring *Bnei-Yisrael* out of Egypt?" he asked (Exod. 3:11). Moses also complained, "ADONAI, I am not a man of words—not yesterday, nor the day before, nor since You have spoken to Your servant—because I have a slow mouth and a heavy tongue" (Exod. 4:10). He even begged, "Lord, please send someone else" (v. 13, NIV).

Talk about a reluctant hero!

But God had a plan for Moses, and he went on to become one of the great heroes in the history of the Jewish people—or, more accurately, one of the greatest heroes in the history of the world. He not only led the Israelites out of Egypt, across the Sinai Peninsula, and into the land God had promised them, but he became a great leader and lawgiver, establishing a system of laws and a moral code that has been a model for every civilized nation over the past four thousand years.

God does not see us as the world sees us. Nor does He see us as we see ourselves. There are two other characters in the Bible who became great heroes despite very humble beginnings. You may be familiar with their stories, but I want to share them with you now because they show clearly that God does not see things the way we do.

Their names? Joseph and David.

The Dreamer

Joseph was the second-youngest of twelve brothers, a dreamer who annoyed his older siblings by telling them about the dreams he had. "There we were binding sheaves in the middle of the field. All of a sudden, my sheaf arose and stood upright. And behold, your sheaves gathered around and bowed down to my sheaf" (Gen. 37:7).

His brothers became so angry by this kind of talk that they sold him into slavery and told their father that he had been killed by a wild animal. Joseph was taken into Egypt, where he was sold to a government official named Potiphar. Falsely accused of sexual assault by Potiphar's wife, he was thrown into prison, where he languished for years. But even in the midst of this trial, he never forgot that he belonged to God, nor that God had a plan for his life.

The Bible says, "But Adonai was with Joseph and extended kindness to him and gave him favor in the eyes of the commander of the prison. The commander of the prison entrusted into Joseph's hand all the prisoners who were in the prison, so that everything that was done there, he was responsible for it. The commander of the prison did not concern himself with anything at all under his care, because Adonai was with him, and Adonai made whatever he did successful" (Gen. 39:21–23).

While he was in prison, Joseph's ability to interpret dreams became known. Consequently, when Pharaoh had a troubling dream that none of his advisors could interpret, Joseph was summoned. It turned out that Pharaoh's dream had to do with a famine that was soon going to fall, not only on Egypt but all across the known world.

Joseph not only put Pharaoh's mind at ease, but he also saved thousands upon thousands of people from death by starvation. A grateful Pharaoh gave Joseph a high position in the Egyptian government—second only to himself—and Joseph's own family was saved from starvation as a result.

And yes, Joseph's dream did come true, as his brothers bowed before him, not recognizing him as the little brother they had sold into slavery years before.

Joseph didn't hold a grudge against his brothers, despite what they had done to him, because he knew that it had all been God's plan. "Don't be afraid," he told them when they realized who he was. "You intended to harm me, but God intended it for good to accomplish what is now being done, the saving of many lives" (Gen. 50:19–20, NIV).

Why did God choose to do such great things through the young man named Joseph? The question becomes more intriguing when we realize that in biblical times it was the oldest son who was regarded with great honor and respect. He was the one who would take over as the family patriarch when his father died. The oldest son was everything. The youngest son was an also-ran. But God doesn't see things the way people do.

Joseph had a loyal heart, an unwavering faith, and a courageous spirit. He trusted God at all times—and God eventually brought him out on top.

And, by the way, Joseph's own father, Jacob, was not a first-born either. According to the laws and customs of the time, his twin brother Esau, older by a few minutes, should have become head of the family upon Isaac's death. But God chose Jacob not only to be head of the family, but to be the father and patriarch of the twelve tribes of Israel. The genealogical line through which the Messiah was born passed through Jacob, not Esau.

And Jacob and Joseph weren't the only last-born sons that God chose to honor in a special way. A young shepherd boy named David was another.

THE GREAT KING

David was the greatest of the kings of ancient Israel. The Bible says he was a man after God's own heart. The psalms he wrote have brought joy to millions of believers around the world.

But when God first chose him to do something great, he was the insignificant baby brother in a family full of strong, handsome young men.

God told the prophet Samuel to go to the house of a man named Jesse. There, God would direct him to anoint one of Jesse's sons as the next king of Israel. One by one the young men came before Samuel. And every time, Samuel thought, "This must be the one." But God always said no. The Bible says:

> Then Samuel asked Jesse, "Are these all the boys you have?"
>
> "There's still the youngest," he replied. "But right now, he's tending the sheep."
>
> "Send and bring him," Samuel said to Jesse, "for we will not sit down until he comes here."
>
> So he sent word and had him come. Now he was ruddy-cheeked, with beautiful eyes and a handsome appearance. Then ADONAI said, "Arise, anoint him, for this is the one."
>
> So Samuel took the horn of oil and anointed him in the midst of his brothers. From that day on Ruach ADONAI

came mightily upon David. Then Samuel rose up and
went to Ramah.

—1 SAMUEL 16:11–13

DAVID AND THE GIANT

Before he ascended to the throne of Israel, David killed a
Philistine warrior named Goliath, who had defied the armies
of Israel. The Bible describes Goliath this way:

> [He was over nine feet tall.] He had a bronze helmet on his
> head and wore a coat of scale armor of bronze weighing
> five thousand shekels; on his legs he wore bronze greaves,
> and a bronze javelin was slung on his back. His spear
> shaft was a like a weaver's rod, and its iron point weighed
> six hundred shekels.

—1 SAMUEL 17:4–7, NIV

In other words, Goliath's armor weighed 125 pounds. The
point of his spear added another 15 pounds. He was a monster
of a man, but David wasn't afraid of him because he believed
God had a great plan for his life. It seems that David was the
only person in the Israelite army who wasn't afraid of Goliath.
And, in fact, David wasn't even in the army, because he was
too young. He had gone to the front, at his father's request, to
check on three of his older brothers.

He discovered that the entire army was being shamed by this
one Philistine warrior. Every morning for forty days, Goliath
had issued the same challenge. "Send one of your men out to
fight me. If he wins, then the Philistines will surrender and be
your slaves. But if I win, then the Israelites must surrender to
us and become our slaves." (See 1 Samuel 17:8–9.)

There wasn't a soldier in the Israelite army who was ready to take that challenge. Instead, they all sat in their tents, quaking in their boots, wishing that someone else would be brave enough to fight the giant. It made David angry to see how Goliath mocked the army of Israel, and it made him feel even worse that no one had the faith or courage to respond to the challenge.

Surprisingly, when the future king indicated that he would be willing to fight the giant, other men put him down, including his own brother, Eliab. The Bible says, "Now when Eliab his oldest brother heard him speaking to the men, Eliab's anger was kindled against David. 'Why have you come down here?' he asked. 'So with whom did you leave those few sheep in the wilderness? I know your insolence and the wickedness of your heart! For you've come down here to watch the battle'" (1 Sam. 17:28). David, of course, was indignant when he heard his brother's comment. "What have I done now?" he asked. "It was only a question!" (v. 29).

Continue in the seventeenth chapter of 1 Samuel, and you'll find David going out to meet Goliath on the field of battle.

> Then David said to the Philistine, "You are coming to me with a sword, a spear and a javelin, but I am coming to you in the Name of ADONAI-Tzva'ot, God of the armies of Israel, whom you have defied. This very day ADONAI will deliver you into my hand, and I will strike you down and take your head off you, and I will give the carcasses of the Philistines' camp today to the birds of the sky and the wild beasts of the earth. Then all the earth will know that there is a God in Israel, and so all this assembly will know that ADONAI delivers not with sword and spear—for the

battle belongs to ADONAI—and He will give you into our hands."

—1 SAMUEL 17:45–47

Goliath laughed when he saw David coming out to meet him in battle. He was only a boy. He wore no armor. Surely he was no match for the giant's strength, power, and battlefield experience.

Goliath isn't laughing anymore.

David wasn't talking trash. He meant what he said, and with God's help he made good on his threat. The Bible says he picked five smooth stones, although he really needed only one. He placed one of them in his sling, whirled it around his head, and let it fly. His aim was perfect.

Although Goliath was covered by armor, and he had a shield bearer walking in front of him, the stone found the only unprotected place on the giant's head. It struck him in the middle of the forehead, and he toppled over, face forward on the ground.

The Bible says that David ran forward, took Goliath's sword from its scabbard, and cut off the giant's head. When the Philistines saw that their champion was dead, they ran in fear, with the Israelites in hot pursuit. "Then the men of Israel and Judah surged forward with a shout and pursued the Philistines to the entrance of Gath and to the gates of Ekron. Their dead were strewn along the Shaaraim road to Gath and Ekron. When the Israelites returned from chasing the Philistines, they plundered their camp" (1 Sam. 17:52–53, NIV).

David won the battle over the giant because he knew who he was in God—no matter what anyone else thought of him.

Goliath saw him as "only a boy," but he saw himself as a mighty warrior.

His older brothers saw him as a brat and a pest, but he saw himself as a vessel of God's power.

His own father was indifferent to him. He didn't even think enough of the boy to introduce him to Samuel when the prophet came searching for the next king of Israel. But David never doubted himself. Not for an instant.

Who Are You?

David knew who he was. Do you know who you are?

I'm not talking about what you've done, where you've been, or what you've experienced. That has nothing to do with who you are in God.

Neither am I talking about the amount of money in your bank account, how good looking you are, or whether you've experienced some failures in life. Instead, I'm talking about what God thinks of you.

The prophet Isaiah writes:

> Should the potter be regarded the same as the clay? Should the thing made say to its maker, "You did not make me"? Or the thing formed say of its former, "You have no understanding"?
> —Isaiah 29:16

Because God made you, you can know that you are something special!

A long time ago, there was a popular poster that said, "I know I'm somebody because God don't make no junk." Yes, the grammar leaves a lot to be desired, but the thought is on target. God doesn't make junk. He formed the dazzling galaxies that fly through space, millions of light years from earth. He formed the snow-capped mountains that rise high into the sky. The vast forests, with their rivers and lakes. The beauty of His creation is all around us. And the creation of humanity was His crowning achievement.

You are fearfully and wonderfully made (Ps. 139:14, NIV). Don't ever forget it.

The way you see yourself can change many things about you. It can reduce stress, attract other people, and improve your performance in many areas of life.

The latter was proven in a study undertaken with a number of top-notch swimmers. Before they participated in the study, the swimmers were asked a number of questions to gauge how they felt about themselves—and life in general. Some were graded as "optimistic," while others fell into the "pessimistic" category. After they swam their trial laps, the coach lied to them about the times they had turned in. They were all told that they had not done as well as they really had, and were urged to try again.

Almost all of those who fell into the optimistic group turned in a better performance the second time around. Those who were pessimistic did worse.[1]

In his book *The Power of Optimism*, Alan Loy McGinnis tells a similar story:

> Dr. George E. Vaillant has been following the physical and mental health of several hundred Harvard graduates since the mid-1940s. The data includes the results of extensive physical exams done every five years from age twenty-five through sixty. Ninety-nine of the men were rated by researchers as pessimistic, and they had markedly more illness between forty-five and sixty than the optimists. Curiously, a man's attitude at age twenty-five does not seem to affect his health for about twenty years. But if he has a robust body and good health at twenty-five and also carries a bleak and cynical attitude,

the researchers can predict that his health will begin to fall apart at middle age.[2]

McGinnis goes on to tell of another far more serious study involving sixty-nine women who had mastectomies for breast cancer.

> Three months after the surgery the women were asked how they viewed the nature and seriousness of the disease and how it had affected their lives. Five years later 75 percent of the women who had reacted with a positive, fighting spirit were alive, whereas less than half of those who reacted either stoically or helplessly were still alive.[3]

Clearly, seeing yourself in a good light pays off. And yet most of us tend to focus on the things about ourselves we don't like.

Leonardo da Vinci once said, "I have offended God and mankind because my work didn't reach the quality it should have."[4]

Really? How could one of the most brilliant and talented men who ever lived see himself that way? Because, as I said, it is human nature. We have to learn to see ourselves in a positive light. And besides, our ancient enemy, Satan, loves it if he can get us to doubt ourselves. He loves it because it makes us weak. And when we're weak, we are easy prey.

As psychologist Alfred Adler said, "To be a human being means to feel oneself inferior."[5] But you're not inferior. Here is just some of what God says about you:

> Therefore, there is now no condemnation for those who are in Messiah *Yeshua*.
>
> —ROMANS 8:1

But in all these things we are more than conquerors through Him who loved us.

—ROMANS 8:37

He chose us in the Messiah before the foundation of the world, to be holy and blameless before Him in love. He predestined us for adoption as sons through Messiah *Yeshua*, in keeping with the good pleasure of His will—to the glorious praise of His grace, with which He favored us through the One He loves! In Him we have redemption through His blood—the removal of trespasses—in keeping with the richness of His grace that He lavished on us.

—EPHESIANS 1:4–8

Therefore if anyone is in Messiah, he is a new creation. The old things have passed away; behold, all things have become new.

—2 CORINTHIANS 5:17

See how glorious a love the Father has given us, that we should be called God's children—and so we are!

—1 JOHN 3:1

GOD'S PROMISES TO YOU

In the midst of this uncertain world, Yeshua also makes a number of important promises we can cling to:

Therefore do not worry, saying, "What will we eat?" or "What will we drink?" or "What will we wear?" For the pagans eagerly pursue all these things; yet your Father in heaven knows that you need all these. But seek first the kingdom of God and His righteousness, and all these things shall be added to you.

—MATTHEW 6:31–33

"Amen, I tell you," *Yeshua* replied, "there is no one who has left house or brothers or sisters or mother or father or children or property, for My sake and for the sake of the Good News, who will not receive a hundred times as much now in this time, houses and brothers and sisters and mothers and children and property, along with persecutions; and in the *olam ha-ba*, eternal life."
—MARK 10:29–30

Give, and it will be given to you—a good measure, pressed down, shaken together, overflowing, will be given into your lap.
—LUKE 6:38

Behold, I am coming soon, and My reward is with Me, to pay back each one according to his deeds.
—REVELATION 22:12

And then there is this beautiful passage from Matthew 5:3–12 (NIV):

Blessed are the poor in spirit, for theirs is the kingdom of heaven. Blessed are those who mourn, for they will be comforted. Blessed are the meek, for they will inherit the earth. Blessed are those who hunger and thirst for righteousness, for they will be filled. Blessed are the merciful, for they will be shown mercy. Blessed are the pure in heart, for they will see God. Blessed are the peacemakers, for they will be called children of God. Blessed are those who are persecuted because of righteousness, for theirs is the kingdom of heaven. Blessed are you when people insult you, persecute you and falsely say all kinds of evil against you because of me. Rejoice and be glad, because great is your reward in heaven, for in the same way they persecuted the prophets who were before you.

Chapter 11

WALK IN OBEDIENCE

*If anyone loves Me, he will keep My word. My Father will love
him, and We will come to him and make Our dwelling with him.*

—JOHN 14:23

OBEDIENCE IS ANOTHER key to obtaining God's blessings on your life. Keeping God's commandments does not guarantee you a trouble-free life. But it does guarantee that God will be there with you, holding your hand in times of trouble—and nothing could possibly be better than that!

There are many things I admire about the Bible, and one of these is that it is painfully honest about the great heroes of faith. We talked about this in chapter 3, where I listed the sins of people like Noah, Abraham, and David.

On the other hand, there are some characters in the Bible who come across as always trusting, always obedient, almost without a flaw. Joseph is one of them. It seems to me that the only thing he ever did wrong was tell his brothers about his dream that they would bow down to him someday. And even then, I don't think he was being proud or arrogant. He was a boy who didn't understand how his brothers would react.

And yet despite the fact that he lived out his life in absolute obedience, Joseph certainly suffered. For years, it almost seemed as if a dark cloud was following him around. I can imagine his friends rolling their eyes and saying, "That Joseph. As far as that guy's concerned, if anything bad can happen, it *will* happen." Sold into slavery. Framed and thrown into prison. Forgotten by the cupbearer who promised to tell Pharaoh about him.

Nevertheless, by the time we get to the end of the story, we see that God was using all of that suffering to put Joseph into position to become one of the greatest world leaders of his time.

Job is another obedient person who suffered a great deal. But as with Joseph, he came out pretty well in the end. The Bible says, "ADONAI doubled everything that Job had before" (Job 42:10).

Obviously there are times when obedience can cause pain, but that pain is always temporary. And as a general rule, the more obedient you are, the more your life will line up with God's perfect will, and the happier you'll be.

COME, FOLLOW ME

Have you ever noticed that Yeshua never begged anyone to follow Him? When He saw Peter and Andrew casting their net into the Sea of Galilee, He simply said, "Follow Me, and I will make you fishers of men" (Matt. 4:18–19).

He never tried to get people to follow Him by promising them all kinds of great rewards—the kind of thing you might hear on a late-night television commercial: "Follow me and you'll have the time of your life, guaranteed. You'll see incredible miracles. You'll feed five thousand people with a few loaves and fishes! You'll see a man walk on water! And wait, there's more…"

He didn't make a single promise that following Him would be fun, lead to fame and fortune, or increase popularity. In fact, on at least a couple of occasions, He was downright discouraging. Matthew 8:19–20 tells of a Torah scholar who came to Jesus and said, "Teacher, I will follow You wherever You go." How did Jesus answer? "Foxes have dens and birds of the air have nests, but the Son of Man has nowhere to lay His head." In other words, "Have you really counted the cost?"

On another occasion, Jesus said, "If anyone wants to follow Me, he must deny himself, take up his cross every day, and follow Me" (Luke 9:23).

The life of the believer is not without disappointment and heartache. Choosing to follow God can be choosing to walk down a lonely road, especially if you are one of very few among your friends or family who are walking in "paths of righteousness." If anyone ever tells you that following God will bring you a life of nonstop comfort and prosperity, tell them to go read the eleventh chapter of Hebrews. There you'll find a long list of people who suffered for their faith.

But please remember that God will work everything together for your ultimate good. He has His eye on the big picture rather than the temporary troubles that cause us all so much grief from time to time.

And remember, too, that even though the path God has charted for you may not be a complete bed of roses, you can be absolutely sure it will be the most fulfilling, exciting, and ultimately rewarding life you could possibly live.

THE FUTURE LOOKS GLORIOUS

As Paul writes, "For I consider the sufferings of this present time not worthy to be compared with the coming glory to be revealed to us" (Rom. 8:18).

An old hymn asks the question:

> Must I be carried to the skies
> On flowery beds of ease,
> While others fought to win the prize,
> And sailed through bloody seas?[1]

The answer to that question is "absolutely not." God cares about you too much to allow you to become a spiritual couch potato. He wants you to be the best person you can possibly be—in mind, body, and spirit.

He always wants the best for us, but He may not agree with us about what's best for us—and He is always right. I may think it's best for me to sleep until noon every day, eat steak and lobster for dinner seven nights a week, topped off with a gallon of ice cream, and avoid anything that even remotely resembles exercise. But God knows that kind of lifestyle would be the worst thing that could possibly happen to me.

What would you think if you saw a father in a grocery store who was giving in to his child's every whim?

The child points at a box of chocolate donuts.

"I want that."

"OK, sweetie." And the donuts are tossed into the shopping cart.

"I want those, too!" the child says, reaching out for a box of sugary cookies.

"Absolutely, honey."

On and on it goes, as the cart fills up with candy, toys, chips, soda, and unhealthy snacks of all kinds.

Would you admire that parent and think, "He's doing a great job of raising that child"?

I don't think so. I have a feeling you'd think, "This man is a disaster as a dad. He's going to spoil that kid rotten."

And you'd be right. A child who is never told no, who feels entitled to feed every desire and indulge every whim, will never be able to function properly in the world. He will never learn to make wise choices or stand on his own feet. If that's the way it is in the realm of the physical, why would we expect it to be any different in the spiritual realm? We shouldn't.

And yet some people think that God exists to cater to our every whim. He's there to make sure we live in the best neighborhoods, drive the most expensive cars, send our kids to the most prestigious schools, ensure that our bank accounts are full of money, and see to it that every stock we've invested in becomes a huge winner.

But why would God want us to become a bunch of self-indulgent brats?

He doesn't. That's why He gives us what we *need* instead of what we *want*.

A Man Named Paul

I began this chapter with a scripture written by the Apostle Paul. What an amazing, powerful man of God he was. He wrote most of the New Testament, and the Gospel of Luke was written by one of his closest associates. He spread the good news about salvation through faith in Yeshua all over the known world, and he was single-handedly responsible for taking the gospel to the non-Jewish world. Talk about one of the great heroes of the Bible! Paul was a spiritual giant. The twenty-eighth chapter of Acts says that when Paul prayed for sick people on the island of Malta, they were all healed.

It's hard to imagine that a man like that ever had a hard day. But the truth is, he had plenty of them. In the eleventh chapter of 2 Corinthians, he says he was:

- Exposed to death again and again
- Given thirty-nine lashes on five separate occasions
- Beaten with rods three times
- Pelted with stones once
- Shipwrecked three times, and spent a night and a day in the open sea

- Deprived of sleep

- Hungry, thirsty, cold, and naked

> I have been in dangers from rivers, dangers from robbers,
> dangers from my countrymen, dangers from the Gentiles,
> dangers in the city, dangers in the desert, dangers in the
> sea, dangers among false brothers, in labor and hardship,
> through many sleepless nights, in hunger and thirst, often
> without food, in cold and exposure.
> —2 CORINTHIANS 11:26–27

We also know from the Scriptures that Paul had what he called "a thorn in the flesh." We don't know for certain what that thorn was, although there is some evidence that points to Paul's eyes. Remember that Paul was transformed when he came face-to-face with the Messiah while traveling to Damascus to persecute believers there. After his encounter with the risen Lord, Paul was blind until Ananias came and prayed for him.

Paul also says to the Galatians, "For I testify that you would have torn out your eyes and given them to me, if possible" (Gal. 4:15). At the end of the Book of Galatians, he writes, "Notice the large letters—I am writing to you with my own hand" (Gal. 6:11).

So again, it seems likely that Paul's "thorn in the flesh" was some residual vision problem, although the Bible does not say for sure. All we know is that whatever the problem was, God did not take it away. Paul writes:

> I pleaded with the Lord three times about this, that it
> might leave me. But He said to me, "My grace is sufficient
> for you, for power is made perfect in weakness." Therefore
> I will boast all the more gladly in my weaknesses, so that
> the power of Messiah may dwell in me. For Messiah's sake,

> then, I delight in weaknesses, in insults, in distresses, in persecutions, in calamities. For when I am weak, then I am strong.
>
> —2 Corinthians 12:8–10

Your life will not be trouble-free. Just before He was crucified, Yeshua told His apostles, "In the world you will have trouble, but take heart! I have overcome the world!" (John 16:33).

But Yeshua also promised to give us peace in the midst of any suffering that comes our way. He promised that He would never leave or forsake us, and that He will be with us until the end of the age. He also promised us joy in the midst of whatever suffering the world tries to throw at us: "Just as the Father has loved Me, I also have loved you. Abide in My love! If you keep My commandments, you will abide in My love, just as I have kept My Father's commandments and abide in His love. These things I have spoken to you so that My joy may be in you, and your joy may be full" (John 15:9–11).

It's so important to understand that God never forgets about you. He's always there for you, offering you a place of refuge and safety, even if it seems like the whole world has turned against you.

The eighth chapter of Matthew tells about a time when Jesus and His disciples were out on the Sea of Galilee in a small boat and a terrible storm blew up. The waves were sweeping over the sides of the little craft and threatened to send it to the bottom of the sea, about one hundred twenty feet below. As the disciples worked frantically to bail out the boat and keep it afloat, they noticed that Jesus was fast asleep.

They were incredulous. How could He be so relaxed in the middle of this life-threatening storm? The Bible says:

So they came and woke Him up, saying, "Master, save us! We're perishing!"

He said to them, "Why are you afraid, O you of little faith?" Then He got up and rebuked the winds and the sea, and it became totally calm.

The men were amazed, saying, "What kind of person is this? Even the winds and the sea obey Him!"

—MATTHEW 8:25–27

No matter what storms may come your way, God is there offering you a place of refuge. He says, "Come to Me, all who are weary and burdened, and I will give you rest. Take My yoke upon you and learn from Me, for I am gentle and humble in heart, and 'you will find rest for your souls.' For My yoke is easy and My burden is light" (Matt. 11:28–30).

Like the psalmist, you have nothing to fear even if you walk through the Valley of the Shadow of Death, because God is there watching over you.

As he wrote in another of his psalms:

God is our refuge and strength, an ever-present help in trouble. Therefore we will not fear, though the earth change, though the mountains topple into the heart of the seas, though its waters roar and foam, though the mountains quake at their swelling.

—PSALM 46:1–3

We've talked about the fact that God is *not* going to spoil His people by catering to our every whim. He knows the difference between what we want and what we need, and He wants us to have the latter. God is not into giving us baubles that turn to dust in our hands and leave us disappointed and bitter. God wants us to have the things that bring lasting satisfaction and joy. There is such a great difference between what He wants for us and the cheap substitute that Satan wants us to strive for.

- God wants us to have love, but Satan tries to trick us into settling for lust.

- God wants us to be contented with what we have, while Satan convinces us that greed is good and we always need more, more, more!

- God wants us to know the satisfaction that comes from an honest day's work, and the sleep that comes from an unsullied conscience. Satan wants us to use other people for personal gain and to keep on the lookout for a shortcut to the top.

- God wants us to have the real thing. Satan wants us to seek after the cheap imitation.

- God's hands are open wide. He wants to give us what is best, but in order to receive what He has for you, you have to know your place in His family.

I heard a story not long ago about a multimillionaire who left his entire fortune—something like $50 million—to his niece. The only problem was that nobody knew where she was. It took three years after the final will was read to track her down.

And all that time, she was homeless on the streets of New York City. She survived on food scraps fished out of dumpsters. Slept in alleyways and under bridges. She dressed in rags that did almost nothing to protect her from the bitter winter cold. Every day was a struggle to survive, because she didn't know that her rich relative had left her a fortune. She could have dined in the finest restaurants in Manhattan and slept in luxury every night. But she settled for garbage and rags because she didn't know any better.

Don't let Satan fool you.

Don't settle for the garbage and rags he wants to give you.

"Do not be afraid, little flock, for your Father chose to give you the kingdom" (Luke 12:32).

As God's plan for you unfolds, you will find that in the midst of life's ups and downs, the peace that passes all understanding will rule in your heart. And as you live in obedience, the fruit of the Spirit will grow in you.

> But the fruit of the Spirit is love, joy, peace, patience, kindness, goodness, faithfulness, gentleness and self-control.
> —GALATIANS 5:22–23, NAS

Think about this for a moment. You'll have a heart full of love, abundant joy, peace that passes all understanding, and patience instead of worry and stress. You'll be a kind, good, faithful, gentle person, in complete control of yourself at all times. What on earth could be better than that?

Even when things go wrong, it's important to realize that this life is only a pale shadow of what awaits us in heaven. The movie *End of the Spear* tells of five young men who believed God was calling them to take the message of God's love to the warlike Auca Indians, who lived in the jungles of Ecuador. As a result of their obedience, all five lost their lives, thrust through with spears and left to die on a sandy riverbank.

But the story didn't end there. Through the efforts of the families those martyrs left behind, the Indians were won to the Lord. They put aside their weapons and made peace with their longtime enemies. An entire region was transformed by

God's love. Jim Elliot, one of the young men who was killed in Ecuador, had written in his journal, "Lord, God, give me a faith that will take sufficient quiver out of me so that I can sing. Over the Aucas Father, I want to sing!"[2]

Years later one of the widows, Olive Fleming Liefeld, returned to Ecuador and met with some of the Indian warriors who had since given their lives to Jesus. As they talked with great sorrow about the day of the massacre, some of the Indians said that singing had been heard after the missionaries had been speared to death.

"Who was singing?" Olive asked.

The Indians replied, "After the men were killed, Dawa in the woods and Kimo on the beach heard singing. As they looked up over the tops of the trees, they saw a large group of people. They were all singing and it looked as if there were a hundred flashlights. And then suddenly the light disappeared."[3]

A translator explained to Olive that "flashlights" was the only word the Indians knew that meant "bright lights."

Olive asked the translator if the Indians could have made up that story because they thought it might please her to know that her husband and the others were rewarded for their sacrifice.

No, the translator replied. He had heard the same story years earlier, dating almost back to the time of the killings—and the accounts had always been amazingly similar. In fact, the two eyewitnesses, Dawa and Kimo, had, from the beginning, agreed on all the details of everything they saw. The story they told now had not altered from what they had told in the 1950s.

From a worldly viewpoint, things had not turned out at all well for Jim Elliot and his friends. But from a heavenly perspective, defeat was swallowed up in glorious victory and joy![4]

JOHN'S STORY

John is a man who started his own business after thirty years as someone else's employee. Coincidentally he became a Christian about the same time he launched out on his own. Since then it seems that John's life has been a high-wire act. On more than one occasion money to cover payroll has come in at the last minute—an answer to intense prayer by John, his wife, Sue, and their employees.

If John were not a believer, life on the edge might be unbearable. He'd have an ulcer, at the very least. But John has learned to look beyond the mess of the moment and trust that God is working everything out according to Romans 8:28.

John walks daily in faith, following God's leading. Like the time he flew across the United States to meet with a potential customer in northern New England. He flew into a small airport in New Hampshire and then drove three hours through a blinding rain in an attempt to make a sale. When he finally reached his location, the potential customer wouldn't even meet with him. The man had been interested and eager over the phone. But now he was not only disinterested, but also hostile.

John had no choice but to get back in his rental car and make the treacherous drive back to his hotel near the airport. Along the way he wondered out loud why he had made this trip. He had prayed about it and been so sure God wanted him to go.

The next day, after boarding the aircraft for his flight home, he settled back in his seat and began to read. A woman sat down in the seat next to him, and he looked up to say hello. He was shocked when he saw the look on her face. Clearly this person was in the grip of agony and grief. Before he could stop himself, he blurted out, "Are you all right? Is something wrong?"

The woman began to pour out her pain and anguish, caused by numerous problems within her family. After listening for a while, John asked, "Have you ever thought of taking all of this to God?"

"I wouldn't know how to begin to do that," came the answer.

Thus began a long conversation about God's love. Before the trip had ended, the two had prayed together and the woman's agony and pain were replaced by a calm joy.

When they reached their destination, John's new friend kept thanking him over and over. "I will never forget you," she told him. "I know God sent you to me." All John could do was shake his head in amazement. He thought God wanted him to go to New Hampshire to make a sale. But what God really wanted him to do was go to New Hampshire to impact a broken heart for Jesus.

Obedience is always a wonderful adventure!

Chapter 12

GOD IS ALWAYS ON TIME

For while we were still helpless, at the right time Messiah died for the ungodly. For rarely will anyone die for a righteous man—though perhaps for a good man someone might even dare to die. But God demonstrates His own love toward us, in that while we were yet sinners, Messiah died for us.

—ROMANS 5:6–8

Have you ever heard anyone say they were caught between the devil and the deep blue sea? The ancient Israelites certainly knew what that was like. Only for them, it wasn't the deep blue sea but the Red Sea. In front of them, the waters of the sea stretched out as far as the eye could see. Behind them, the entire Egyptian army was bearing down on them.

The Israelites' eyes were wide with terror as they saw the dust clouds being kicked up by the horses and chariots that were racing in their direction. What could they do? If they ran forward into the sea, they'd drown. If they stayed where they were, or turned back, the Egyptians would soon be upon them and they would be slaughtered. It seemed they were doomed.

"Moses!" they screamed. "Did you bring us out into the desert to die?"

The Bible says, "But Moses said to the people, 'Don't be afraid! Stand still, and see the salvation of Adonai, which He will perform for you today. You have seen the Egyptians today, but you will never see them again, ever!" (Exod. 14:13).

God told Moses what to do:

> Then Moses stretched out his hand over the sea. Adonai drove the sea back with a strong east wind throughout the night and turned the sea into dry land. So the waters were divided. Then Bnei-Yisrael went into the midst of the sea on the dry ground, while the waters were like walls to them on their right and on their left.
>
> —Exodus 14:21–22

Do you remember what happened after that? The Egyptians pursued the Israelites into the middle of the Red Sea, but the waters came back together and "covered the chariots and horsemen— the entire army of Pharaoh that had followed the Israelites into the sea. Not one of them survived" (Exod. 14:28, NIV).

The Israelites came within a few minutes of being wiped off the face of the earth. But at just the right moment, when it seemed certain that doom was upon them, God reached down and saved them! It was one of the most thrilling narrow escapes in history.

When you were a child, did you like to watch western movies? I did. The good guys would always get themselves into terrible trouble. There didn't seem to be any way out. And then suddenly the cavalry would come charging to the rescue, flags flying and bugles blaring. What a thrill! I was always so excited I couldn't sit still.

Now, of course those were only movies. But one of the many things I've learned during my long walk with God is that He's a lot like that cavalry. He's always on time, and there is no bad guy—or bad guys—anywhere who can stand up to Him.

JUST IN THE NICK OF TIME

As He did with the Israelites, God often seems to come through at the very last moment, when there is no other way out. That's one of the ways He helps us build faith. He wants us to learn to trust Him in all circumstances.

Now a lot of people have gotten themselves into serious trouble because they got impatient with God. He hadn't done something they wanted Him to do, so they decided to help Him out a little bit, give Him a push in the right direction—and tragedy resulted. Some have rushed into disastrous marriages because they didn't spend time seeking God's will in the matter. Churches have been destroyed because pastors have launched huge capital campaigns without ever considering whether it was what God wanted them to do. Good men have lost everything because they ran ahead of God and got themselves into a world of hurt and trouble.

There is nothing really new about this. Turn back to the Book of Genesis and read the story of Abraham and Sarah. In the twelfth chapter of that book, God promises Abraham that he is going to be the father of many nations. The problem was that Sarah was well past childbearing age and had never had any children. How then was it possible that Abraham was going to become the father of nations?

Sarah had an idea. She decided that Abraham should father a child through her Egyptian maidservant, Hagar. Abraham apparently thought it was a pretty good idea, so he did as his wife suggested. He slept with Hagar, who became pregnant and gave birth to a boy. They named him Ishmael.

The problem was, that wasn't what God wanted. Sarah and Abraham had run ahead of God instead of waiting on His timing, and their disobedience had far-reaching negative consequences. Sarah became pregnant, even in her advanced age, and gave birth to a boy. They named him Isaac.

She was happy, but she was also jealous of Hagar. She thought Ishmael was picking on Isaac. She was so upset about it, in fact, that she ordered Abraham to send them away.

So it was that Isaac became the father of the Jewish people and Ishmael became the father of the Arabic people. And for thousands of years Arabs and Jews have struggled to coexist. They are brothers who can't seem to get along. Think of the blood that has been shed in the wars that have been fought between Arabs and Jews—the terrorist attacks that continue to constantly rock the Middle East today.

I am not saying it would have been better for the world if Ishmael had never been born, but rather that there is a price to pay for disobedience. It was not God's plan for Ishmael to come into the world at the time and in the way he did, and the world has been paying for it ever since. The Bible tells us to "wait on the Lord," and that's exactly what we need to do. Isaiah 30:18 (NIV) tells us:

> Yet the LORD longs to be gracious to you; therefore he will rise up to show you compassion. For the LORD is a God of justice. Blessed are all who wait for him!

When the Israelites were on their long journey from Egypt to the Promised Land, God sent them a cloud to lead them during the day and a pillar of fire to lead them by night. When the cloud or pillar stood still, the Israelites stayed right where they were. But when the cloud or pillar moved, the Israelites moved too. Any time, day or night, if the cloud began to move, the Israelites were expected to pack their tents and move. That is exactly the way God expects His people to respond to Him today. We must understand that our times are in His hands. Our minutes and hours belong to Him, and they must be surrendered to Him.

I like what pastor and best-selling author Calvin Miller says:

> Of all the gifts God gives us, surely the most precious is the gift of time.
>
> Seconds, minutes, years are all life-parts, assembled and ready for our use in his service. The sand of our lives is running through the hourglass—fast, steady, precious. It is so precious that when we give it back to God, it sets the angels at their alleluias. Yet we cannot give our entire

lives to God at one time and have it done with for all time. We must surrender second by second.[1]

Miller adds:

We cannot possibly flatter the Almighty by hurrying into his presence, flinging a song and a prayer at him, and hurrying out of church back into our hassled lifestyles. God is never flattered by our sanctified exhaustion.[2]

Miller says of Paul:

The apostle understood that only those who obey in the moment can link their obedient moments into a significant lifetime. The point is not to merely live a long time (oat bran and a regimen of herbs will help see to that.). The point is that we are to offer our days as a sacrifice of silver on an altar of gold.[3]

HOW THE IDOLS FELL IN HAWAII

I recently heard the story of how Christianity spread throughout the Hawaiian Islands in the mid-1800s. Once again, all I could do was marvel at how God works things out at just the right time in order to enlarge the borders of His kingdom.

Prior to the mid-nineteenth century, the people of Hawaii worshipped a variety of gods—all of whom were represented by idols. To disobey those gods, or to break any of their taboos, was sure to bring swift and utter destruction. One of those taboos was that women and men were not to eat with each other. Men were served and ate first. Women ate when the men were finished. They could not even use the same plates or cups. The lesson, obviously, was that women were inferior to men and were expected to know their place. But when King Kamehameha passed away, his free-spirited son Liholiho ascended to the throne. Liholiho liked to party and didn't care much for the old gods or their taboos. The queen dowager, Kaahumanu, who was actually the power behind the throne, also hated the taboos, primarily because she felt they degraded women.

Early in his reign, just as the first Christian missionaries from the United States were sailing from the East Coast on their way to Hawaii, Liholiho threw a great feast, inviting hundreds of the most powerful people from throughout the islands. Then, spurred on by Kaahumanu, and fortified by alcohol, he did something that shook the people to the core. As they watched in horror, he walked straight to one of the women's tables. The fear in the room was palpable as he sat down with them.

In his classic work *Roughing It* Mark Twain explains what happened next:

> They saw him eat from the same vessel with them, and were appalled! Terrible moments drifted slowly by, and still the king ate, still he lived, still the lightnings of the insulted gods were withheld! Then conviction came like a revelation—the superstitions of a hundred generations passed from before the people like a cloud, and a shout went up, "The *tabu* is broken! The *tabu* is broken!"
>
> Thus did King Liholiho...preach the first sermon and prepare the way for the new gospel that was speeding southward over the waves of the Atlantic.[4]

Most of these people had feared the gods all their lives. They had always believed that one false step would lead to their annihilation. But now that they saw their king freely breaking one of the strongest taboos without the slightest punishment, they decided that the gods were frauds. There was no power in them. They were nothing more than idols carved out of wood.

The angry people surged forward, pulled the idols down, and began to hack them into pieces. Some tried to protect the ancient gods, but they were outnumbered and easily overcome. As for the gods, they did absolutely nothing to protect themselves. Many of the once-feared idols were burned on the spot.

A few days later the pagan priests managed to raise up an army to defend the disgraced gods. They intended to attack the capitol, overthrow the king, and restore the gods to their rightful place of honor. Liholiho sent one of his officials to try to reason with them, but they refused to lay down their arms.

According to Mark Twain:

> So the king sent his men forth under Major-General Kalaimoku and the two hosts met at the Kuamoo. The battle was long and fierce—men and women fighting side by side, as was the custom—and when the day was done the rebels were flying in every direction in hopeless panic, and idolatry and the *tabu* were dead in the land!
>
> The royalists marched gaily home to Kailua glorifying the new dispensation. "There is no power in the gods," said they; "they are a vanity and a lie. The army with idols was weak; the army without idols was strong and victorious!"
>
> The nation was without a religion.
>
> The missionary ship arrived in safety shortly afterward, timed by providential exactness to meet the emergency, and the gospel was planted as in a virgin soil.[5]

It took many weeks for the first missionaries to reach the islands. They had to sail all the way down the east coast of South America, through the treacherous waters of Cape Horn, and then thousands of miles west and north to Hawaii. Even so, their timing was perfect. When they arrived, they found people ready to hear about the God who loved them so much He sent His only Son to die for them. The old gods had been swept away. There was no opposition to the gospel, which swept across the island like a welcome breeze. What an amazing story!

GOD IS ALWAYS IN CONTROL

The Bible is full of other examples of God's mastery over time. In the twenty-second chapter of Genesis, we find that God tested Abraham's faith by telling him to take Isaac into the wilderness and sacrifice him as a burnt offering. Abraham's faith never wavered. He didn't say, "But, Lord, You promised me that a mighty nation was going to come through Isaac." Instead, he took his only son out into the wilderness, as God had told him to do, and prepared to offer him up to God:

> Then they came to the place about which God had told him, and Abraham built the altar there, laid out the wood, bound up Isaac his son, and laid him on the altar, on top of the wood. Then Abraham reached out his hand and took the knife to slaughter his son.
>
> But the angel of ADONAI called to him from heaven and said, "Abraham! Abraham!" He said, "Hineni!" Then He said, "Do not reach out your hand against the young man—do nothing to him at all. For now I know that you are one who fears God—you did not withhold your son, your only son, from Me." Then Abraham lifted up his eyes and behold, there was a ram, just caught in the thick bushes by its horns. So Abraham went and took the ram, and offered it up as a burnt offering instead of his son.
>
> —GENESIS 22:9–13

Once again, God came through in the nick of time and spared Abraham and Isaac from unnecessary grief and suffering.

God also used a young woman named Esther to save the Jewish people from a plot devised by an evil man named Haman. Her uncle, Mordecai, who asked her to put her own life at risk to help save her people, told her, "Who knows but that you have come to royal position for such a time as this?" (Esther 4:14, NIV). Once again, God's divine sense of timing is in evidence. He raised Esther up and made her a queen of Persia so that she could save the Jews at just the right time.

The same thing happened with Joseph. Think of everything Joseph went through. He was sold into slavery by his jealous brothers. He was falsely accused of attempted rape by Potiphar's wife. He spent years in an Egyptian prison. He was a good, morally upright man who loved God, and yet he suffered terribly.

But even here, God's sense of timing was in play. God was refining and preparing Joseph to become one of the most powerful leaders in the world of that day. At the right time, God used Joseph to devise a plan that would save Egypt and many of her neighbors from death by famine. Without Joseph's heroics, millions of Egyptians would have died, as would the entire Hebrew race. Without the food they obtained in Egypt, Joseph's father and brothers would almost certainly have starved to death. That would have been the end of the Jews, the people through whom the Messiah was to come.

Consider Jonah, who was thrown into the sea during a terrible storm. God provided a great fish to swallow Jonah, and Jonah was inside the fish for three days and three nights. That fish had to be in exactly the right place at exactly the right time. Otherwise, Jonah would have drowned. End of story.

You can always trust God's timing. If something doesn't seem to be going your way, turn it over to Him and trust Him to make things come out exactly as they should at exactly the right time.

YESHUA CAME AT THE RIGHT TIME

I believe that God sent His Son, Yeshua, into the world at exactly the right time. Furthermore, I believe that He will return to this world at exactly the right time to reign in power and glory. My friend, author Michael Brown, writes, "The Messiah first came to make peace between God and man, bringing the hope of reconciliation and forgiveness to the world. The ultimate effects of his first coming will lead to his return and an era of complete peace on earth."[6]

The first time the Messiah came into the world, He came in the form of the suffering servant the prophet Isaiah talks about in the fifty-third chapter of the book that bears His name:

> Who has believed our message and to whom has the arm of the LORD been revealed? He grew up before him like a tender shoot, and like a root out of dry ground. He had no beauty or majesty to attract us to him, nothing in his appearance that we should desire him. He was despised and rejected by mankind, a man of suffering, and familiar with pain. Like one from whom people hide their faces he was despised, and we held him in low esteem.
>
> Surely he took up our pain and bore our suffering, yet we considered him punished by God, stricken by him, and afflicted. But he was pierced for our transgressions, he was crushed for our iniquities; the punishment that brought us peace was on him, and by his wounds we are healed. We all, like sheep, have gone astray, each of us has

turned to our own way; and the LORD has laid on him the iniquity of us all.

He was oppressed and afflicted, yet he did not open his mouth; he was led like a lamb to the slaughter, and as a sheep before its shearers is silent, so he did not open his mouth. By oppression and judgment he was taken away. Yet who of his generation protested? For he was cut off from the land of the living; for the transgression of my people he was punished. He was assigned a grave with the wicked, and with the rich in his death, though he had done no violence, nor was any deceit in his mouth.

—ISAIAH 53:1–9, NIV

When Yeshua returns to the world, He will come as the King of kings and Lord of lords. Then:

Then I will pour out on the house of David and the inhabitants of Jerusalem a spirit of grace and supplication, when they will look toward Me whom they pierced. They will mourn for him as one mourns for an only son and grieve bitterly for him, as one grieves for a firstborn.

—ZECHARIAH 12:10

And:

For this reason God highly exalted Him and gave Him the name that is above every name, that at the name of Yeshua every knee should bow, in heaven and on the earth and under the earth, and every tongue profess that YESHUA the Messiah is Lord—to the glory of God the Father.

—PHILIPPIANS 2:9–11

Some who refuse to accept Jesus as the Messiah say that they are bothered by the fact that He came at such a "backward" time in world history. "If He came today," they say, "He would be on every television station around the world. Billions of people would see His miracles and hear His preaching. There wouldn't be any doubt that He was the Messiah."

Well, to begin with, that's not the way the kingdom of heaven takes root and grows. Jesus said it's like a tiny seed that sprouts and grows into a mighty tree, and that's exactly what happened. What began as a movement consisting of thirteen people—Yeshua and the twelve apostles—has reached around the world and gathered more than two billion people into its loving embrace.

So, did the Messiah come at the right time? Listen to this from Michael Brown:

> According to [a] well-known Jewish tradition, the Messiah was supposed to come about two thousand years ago! As explained by [the great rabbi] Rashi, "After the 2,000 years of Torah, it was God's decree that the Messiah would come and the wicked kingdom would come to an end and the subjugation of Israel would be destroyed." Instead, because Israel's sins were many, "the Messiah has not come to this very day..."
>
> Let's take a closer look at the actual dates involved. Most traditional Jews follow Rashi's dating, putting the expected time of the Messiah's arrival at roughly 240 CE [AD]. However, Rashi based his figures on a significant chronological error in the Talmudic tradition, probably the most famous error of its kind in Rabbinic literature. It is a miscalculation of almost two hundred years! You see, when the Scriptures were not explicit in dating times and events, the rabbis had to rely on other sources and traditions to figure out how long certain periods were, sometimes getting these historical periods wrong. In the case in point, they believed that the Second Temple stood for only 420 years, whereas it stood for approximately 600

years. Adjusting Rashi's calculations by roughly 180 years, therefore, we find ourselves in the very century in which Yeshua came to our people. *He* was the one who came in the century in which the Messiah was expected...and this according to a *Rabbinic* tradition.[7]

GOD HOLDS TIME IN HIS HANDS

As we've already discussed, God exists outside of time. He is not limited or bound by it the way human beings are. He is capable of seeing everything at once, while we can only see the past and the present. In other words, unless God reveals it to us through His Word or through the gift of prophecy, we have no idea what will happen in the future. But God knows it all. He is never surprised but knows exactly how and when to act to ensure that everything works together for the good of those who love Him (Rom. 8:28).

Perhaps you have heard of a Chinese author and pastor by the name of Watchman Nee. His books such as *The Normal Christian Life* and *Sit, Walk, Stand* have sold millions of copies all over the world. Nee, who died in 1972, spent the last twenty years of his life in prison. He was responsible for starting thousands of house churches in China. He helped light a flame in that country that is still burning brightly, despite the fact that the Communist government has been trying to extinguish it for over sixty-five years.

Nee was a teenager when he became a follower of Jesus. Shortly after that he and several other enthusiastic young believers sailed to the island of Mei-hwa to share the gospel. They preached for days but didn't get a single response.

The villagers seemed devoted to their local god, Ta-Wang. They explained to the missionaries that on January 11, which was only a few days away, the whole island would come together to celebrate a festival in Ta-Wang's honor. They also reported, proudly, that it had not rained on the day of the festival for nearly three hundred years. When he heard this, one of Watchman Nee's friends retorted, "I promise you, our God, who is the true God, will make it rain on January 11."[8]

Many of those who heard him laughed at him. But they also agreed that if it did rain on that date, they would listen to what the young people had to say about Jesus.

Watchman Nee wasn't happy about what his friend had done. God was under no obligation to make it rain on January 11. He wondered if they were guilty of putting Him to the test. But as he prayed about the situation, he felt that God wanted them to spread the word that He *was* going to make it rain on January 11. So that's exactly what they did.

But when he got out of bed on January 11, he took a look at the sky and wondered for a moment if he had heard wrong. It was a bright, sunny day, with no storm clouds in sight.

At breakfast, Nee and his friends prayed, "Father, please accept our prayer as a gentle reminder."[9] As they were praying, they heard the first drops of rain falling on the roof. Within a few minutes, the few sprinkles had become a downpour.

After the storm the high priest announced that he had made a mistake in his calculations. The festival, he said, was actually supposed to take place on January 14 instead of January 11. Therefore, he claimed that it still hadn't rained on the day of the festival. The Christians had proved nothing. He insisted it would not rain on January 14, and everyone would see that Ta-Wang was the true God.

Over the next three days Watchman Nee and his friends continued to pray that it would rain on the festival day—and during that time, thirty villagers chose to follow Yeshua.

January 14 was almost an exact copy of the eleventh. The day started out bright and sunny, but then a huge storm rolled in, and rain drenched the island. Over the next few weeks, a thriving church was established there. Even though the pagan priest had tried to change the time and the ground rules on God, He came through, just as He said He would.[10]

William J. and Randy Petersen tell Watchman Nee's story in their book *100 Amazing Answers to Prayer.* The book is filled with such faith-lifting accounts.

God's timing is always perfect. You can count on it.

Don't let regrets over your past mistakes stop you from living life to the fullest. There's an old story about a mule that fell into an abandoned well. The animal's owner tried everything he could think of to get that mule out of the well, but nothing worked.

Finally he decided that he was going to bring in a truckload of dirt and pour it into that well. He would bury that old mule and put it out of its misery. He enlisted some neighbors to help him, and they all began shoveling dirt into the well.

Naturally, the animal didn't like it when that first load of dirt landed on his back. But after a moment, he shook it off and stepped on top of it. He did the same when the second load hit him. And the third. And the fourth. All the while, he was getting closer and closer to the top of that well. Finally, he reached the point where he simply stepped out of the well and was free. Like that mule, we must all learn to shake off our past failures and learn from them.

WHAT IF THE RESCUE NEVER COMES?

You may be reading this and asking, "But what about the times when the cavalry doesn't come riding to the rescue just in the nick of time? What about people who die at an early age in car crashes or from diseases like cancer? And what about those times when the mortgage is overdue and the money to pay it never comes?"

I'm certainly not going to deny that such things happen. Remember that Yeshua told us we would have trouble in this world.

When the Israelites were first taken into exile in Babylon, they felt certain that it wouldn't be very long until they would return to the Promised Land. Surely God would come to their rescue. There were even a number of false prophets among them who assured them that they would soon be going home. Then Jeremiah sent them this letter:

> Thus says ADONAI-Tzva'ot, the God of Israel, to all those in captivity, whom I removed as captives into exile from Jerusalem to Babylon: "Build houses and live in them; also plant gardens and eat their fruit; take wives and have sons and daughters; and take wives for your sons and give your daughters to husbands, so that they may bear sons and daughters; and multiply there, and do not decrease. Also seek the shalom of the city where I took you as captives in exile, and pray to ADONAI for it—for in its shalom will you have shalom." For thus says ADONAI, the God of Israel: "Do not let your prophets who are among you or your diviners beguile you, and pay no attention to the dreams which you make them keep dreaming. For they prophesy falsely to you in My Name; I have not sent them." It is a declaration of ADONAI.
>
> —JEREMIAH 29:4–9

Yes, God would bring the Jews back to the Promised Land—but in His own time. There are times when He expects us to make the best of a difficult situation and strive to bloom where we are planted. In every situation there is something important to be learned, something to refine our character and increase our spiritual strength.

Eugene H. Peterson says:

> Jeremiah's letter is a rebuke and a challenge: "Quit sitting around feeling sorry for yourselves. The aim of the person of faith is not to be as comfortable as possible but to live as deeply and thoroughly as possible—to deal with the reality of life, discover truth, create beauty, act out love...The only place you have to be human is where you are right now. The only opportunity you will ever have to live by faith is in the circumstances you are provided this very day: this house you live in, this family you find yourself in, this job you have been given, the weather conditions that prevail at this moment."
>
> Exile (being where we don't want to be with people we don't want to be with) forces a decision: Will I focus my attention on what is wrong with the world and feel sorry for myself? Or will I focus my energies on how I can live at my best in this place I find myself?[11]

An ancient Jewish parable tells of an old man, nearly one hundred years old, who was seen planting a fig tree near his home. Neighbors laughed at him because they knew he would never live long enough to enjoy the figs that tree produced.

When they asked him why he worked so hard to do something that would never benefit him, he replied that he had enjoyed the fruit from trees planted by past generations, now he was planting trees that would provide food for many generations to come.

I believe that's how God expects us to behave. He wants us to do everything we can to make this world a better place, even if we think the world won't last that long.

No matter what happens, we can know that everything is in God's hands and will happen according to His perfect timing. This is true even when we face uncertainty and walk through the valley of the shadow of death.

For example, the Bible says in Hebrews 9:27 that "it is appointed for men to die once, and after this judgment." In other words, "Everyone is going to die sometime." Psalm 39:4 adds, "Let me know, ADONAI, my end and what the number of my days is. Let me know how short-lived I am." And Psalm 139:16 adds, "Your eyes saw me when I was unformed, and in Your book were written the days that were formed—when not one of them had come to be."

If you belong to God and have committed yourself to Him, then you can trust that your life is in His hands. You won't leave this planet one day earlier than God has ordained, nor will you stay here one day longer. In Matthew 6:25–27, Yeshua says, "So I say to you, do not worry about your life—what you will eat or drink, or about your body, what you will wear. Isn't life more than food and the body more than clothing? Look at the birds of the air. They do not sow or reap or gather into barns; yet your Father in heaven feeds them. Are you not of more value than they? And which of you by worrying can add a single hour to his life?"

All we can do regarding this matter is to trust God and know that He will work everything out for our eternal benefit. And it's important to keep an eternal perspective. For the believer, death is not the end, but a glorious new beginning.

An acquaintance told me that she had a vivid dream in which she was sitting around in heaven with a group of friends and family members who were all talking and laughing about how they died. I like that. Viewed from the safety of Yeshua's arms, even death is something to be laughed at rather than feared.

Chapter 13

WHEN YOUR PLAN AND GOD'S PLAN DON'T MATCH

The heart of man plans his course, but ADONAI directs his steps.

—PROVERBS 16:9

I KNOW A MAN—I'LL call him Richard—who grew up thinking he was going to be pastor of a church.

It was his parents' dream. They dedicated him to God when he was still in the womb.

When he was a boy, his parents did everything they could to help him move in the right direction. He attended Christian schools. He was active in his church from a very young age. As a teenager, he was leader of the youth group.

He went on to college, then seminary, and took a job as pastor of a church.

And he hated it.

He loved the Lord, but he just didn't feel cut out to be in ministry. He didn't like to preach. He felt uncomfortable and tongue-tied when he went to check on members of his church who were hospitalized or homebound. He was impatient dealing with the church's bureaucracy.

He was nearly thirty years old when he discovered that the dream he had always thought was his wasn't really his at all. He had spent his whole life following his parents' dream.

He had always assumed he was doing what God wanted him to. He'd never questioned it. If he had taken a close look at it, he might have discovered that God had gifted him in other areas. Please understand that I believe there is no higher calling than the ministry. But at the same time, it *is* a calling that doesn't come to everyone.

Thankfully for Richard, he was smart enough to do something about it. He could have stayed where he was, but he probably would have been miserable for the rest of his life. Instead, he moved into another field where he was able to use his God-given skills and interests, and he has a happy and successful life and career.

Richard discovered that the plans we make for ourselves don't always line up with God's plans for us. Whenever that happens, we always need to trust Him and know that His plan for us is better than anything we might have devised on our own. That's not to say that God's plan will be revealed to us all at once. It may be uncovered one step at a time. Dietrich Bonhoeffer wrote that one mark of the true disciple is that he doesn't know where he's going—only that he is following Jesus.

As I've already mentioned, when I went off to the University of Buffalo, my goal was to make lots of money. I wanted to be a millionaire by the time I was thirty, and I hoped my degree in business would get me there.

Obviously God had other plans for me. After I had an encounter with Him, I switched my major from business to theology. I made a complete U-turn. I no longer cared about making a fortune, because I learned there is something to life that is far more important than money. As Jesus said, "For what does it profit a man to gain the whole world, yet forfeit his soul?" (Mark 8:36).

I did not fulfill my goal of becoming a millionaire by the time I was thirty—but I wouldn't trade what I found for a *billion* dollars. When I look back at what was important to me in those days, I can hardly believe it. It breaks my heart to think that some people never grow beyond the desire for worldly success.

At the time I knew that God's plan for me was to go into some type of ministry. But I didn't know the specifics. I didn't know that I'd spend time in Russia or Israel...or that I'd have the privilege of sharing God's love with people all over the world. And, of course, I didn't know that I would become president of

Jewish Voice Ministries International, because I did not even know Jewish Voice existed at that time. All I can say is that the plans God had for me were far better than any plans I could have devised for myself, and you can be sure that the same is true of you.

YOU WANT ME TO DO WHAT?

What if God asks you to do something that seems to be beneath the talents and ability He has given you? Do it, and He will lift you up!

The fifth chapter of 2 Kings tells the story of Naaman, a mighty man who served as commander of the army of the king of Aram. The Bible says he "was a great man in the sight of his master and highly esteemed" (v. 1, NIV).

Yet Naaman had a terrible problem. He had contracted leprosy. There was no cure for this disease and he knew it. Furthermore, people who had leprosy were isolated from their families and communities. They were cut off from everyone they loved because their illness was thought to be so contagious and dangerous.

But then Naaman heard there was a prophet in Israel named Elisha who had the power to cure him. This represented his one and only hope. Naaman went to his king, who said, "By all means, go" (v. 5, NIV). So Naaman "went with his horses and chariots and stopped at the door of Elisha's house" (v. 9, NIV).

Naaman was accustomed to getting plenty of respect wherever he went. He was the type of fellow you didn't mess around with. For this reason, he was more than a little offended and disappointed when Elisha sent a messenger to him who told him, "Go, wash yourself seven times in the Jordan, and your flesh will be restored and you will be cleansed" (v. 10).

"What?" Naaman thought. "Wash myself in the tiny, muddy Jordan River? He's got to be kidding. The rivers back home are a lot better than this one."

God had spoken through the prophet and told Naaman what he had to do to be healed, but Naaman didn't like God's plan. It wasn't flashy and exciting enough for a man of his stature. He wanted flash and sizzle, not a bath in a muddy river.

The Bible says, "Naaman was angered and walked away, saying, 'I thought he would surely come out to me, stand and call on the Name of ADONAI his God, and wave his hand over the spot and cure the tza'arat [leprosy]'" (v. 11). He was so upset that he turned and went off in a rage.

Fortunately for Naaman, some of his servants were bold enough to talk some sense into him. "My father, if the prophet had told you to do something difficult, would you not have done it? How much more then, when he told you only to 'Wash and be clean'?" (v. 13).

He had to admit, they were right.

Naaman humbled himself, went down and washed himself seven times in the Jordan as the prophet had told him to do, and "his flesh was restored and became clean like that of a young boy."

If Naaman had not done what God told him to do, he would have spent the rest of his life separated from his family and community, and leprosy would eventually have taken his life. If God's plan for you seems to be a letdown, remember this: "Whoever exalts himself shall be humbled, and whoever humbles himself shall be exalted" (Matt. 23:12).

As Hebrews 11:24–26 says, "By faith Moses, when he had grown up, refused to be called the son of Pharaoh's daughter. Instead he chose to suffer mistreatment along with the people of God, rather than to enjoy the passing pleasures of sin. He considered the disgrace of Messiah as greater riches than the treasures of Egypt—because he was looking ahead to the reward."

James 4:17 tells us, "Therefore whoever knows the right thing to do and does not do it—for him it is sin." Disobedience may bring false pleasure that is temporary and passes quickly. Following God's plan brings lasting satisfaction and pleasure.

A GIRL NAMED JONI

Joni Eareckson Tada knows all about what happens when our own plans don't line up with God's plans for us. The last of four daughters born into a strongly Christian family in Baltimore, Joni grew into an active, outgoing teenager who loved outdoor sports like swimming, hiking, and horseback riding. She was a bright young lady with seemingly unlimited potential. She was beautiful, intelligent, and talented. Joni was an excellent artist and singer. There was very little she could not do.

Then in July of 1967, when she was just seventeen years old, she was paralyzed from the shoulders down when she broke her neck in a diving accident. It seemed that all of her dreams were shattered. So many of her favorite activities depended on the strength of her arms and legs, and now she couldn't move them at all.

She went through two years of rehabilitation. By her own admission, she was often angry, had suicidal thoughts, and entertained serious doubts about the religious faith that had always been an important part of her life.

Over time she decided that she had a choice to make. She could give up and live in doubt and fear—or she could believe that God still had a plan for her life, and begin pushing herself to the limits of her ability, just as she had always done before her accident.

As she began letting go of her regrets about the past and looking forward to the future, her doubts about God's love and existence began to disappear.

Remarkably Joni learned how to paint by holding a brush between her teeth. It's an understatement to say it wasn't easy. As you can imagine, there were many setbacks along the way. Joni wouldn't settle for "good enough." She was determined to make sure that the paintings she did with the brush clenched between her teeth were every bit as good as those she had done with her hands. It took hours, days, and weeks of hard work, but she finally got there. Her strikingly beautiful artwork won the praise of critics everywhere and began selling all over the world.

At this time, Joni also began working on her autobiography. The book, *Joni*, was published in 1976, became an immediate best seller, and was made into a motion picture, starring Joni as herself. A second book, *A Step Further*, was published in 1978. In 1982, she married Ken Tada, and they are still happily married to each other.

Despite her traumatic, life-changing injury, Joni has lived an amazingly full life. And through everything she has done, she has sought to share the love of God and bring others into His kingdom.

Of course, nobody wants to go through life as a quadriplegic. I'm sure that Joni would give just about anything to go back to 1967 and relive the day of her accident. She would stay far away from the Chesapeake Bay and the dive that altered her life forever.

Even so, the terrible accident she endured didn't end her life. Instead, it opened the doors to all kinds of exciting possibilities. She has written more than forty books, recorded a number of top-selling musical albums, been a popular radio host, and is an advocate for disabled people through an organization called Joni and Friends that she founded.

I won't go into all the awards and honors she has received, but there are plenty of them.

You may be wondering why a loving God would allow a seventeen-year-old girl with amazing potential to break her neck diving into the Chesapeake Bay. I'm afraid I don't have an answer to that. I don't believe it was something God wanted to happen. Perhaps for some reason it was unavoidable. But what I do know is that when Joni trusted God and allowed Him to make the most of the situation, He did exactly that. Remember Romans 8:28: "Now we know that all things work together for good for those who love God."

Chapter 14

DON'T FORGET GOD WHEN ALL IS WELL

Bless ADONAI, O my soul, and forget not all His benefits:
He forgives all your iniquity. He heals all your diseases.
He redeems your life from the Pit. He crowns you with
lovingkindness and compassions. He satisfies your years with
good things, so that your youth is renewed like an eagle.

—PSALM 103:2–5

I N THE TWELFTH chapter of Luke, Jesus tells a parable about a man who had it all together. Or at least he thought he did.

All of his hard work had paid off. His fields were bursting with nutritious crops, and his barns were full. His only problem was finding room to store all the riches God had given him. As he thought about it one night, he came up with what seemed to him to be a wonderful idea.

> Here's what I'll do! I'll tear down my barns and build larger ones, and there I'll store all my grain and my goods. And I'll say to myself, "O my soul, you have plenty of goods saved up for many years! So take it easy! Eat, drink, and be merry."
>
> —Luke 12:18–19

But what did God think about all this? He called the rich farmer a fool. "Tonight your soul is being demanded back from you! And what you have prepared, whose will that be?" (v. 20).

Jesus went on to say, "So it is with the one who stores up treasure for himself and is not rich in God" (v. 21).

Have you ever noticed that it's often easier to trust and obey God when life isn't going well? When things are good, people tend to start thinking they are self-reliant and put their faith on the back burner. God allowed foreign nations to carry the children of Israel into captivity because they had forgotten His laws and turned their backs on Him.

We must never forget that we are dependent on God's love and mercy—*all* the time.

It's also important to remember that success in this life is not necessarily a sign that God is blessing us. God does not view success in the same way we do. The Bible is very clear on this, although there is still quite a bit of confusion on the subject. Before continuing on, I must add that there is nothing particularly "spiritual" about poverty either. Some people are poor because they have spent their money recklessly, or because they have not obeyed the Bible's commands to be diligent and work hard, or because they have failed to plan ahead. Others are poor because they have given their money away to help others in need. So again, neither wealth nor poverty is a sign of spiritual strength or weakness. Only God knows, and only He can judge.

Jesus's disciples were shocked when He told them that it was easier for a camel to pass through the eye of a needle than for a rich man to enter into heaven (Matt. 19:24).

Their jaws dropped and they asked, "Who then can be saved?" (v. 25, NIV).

Jesus responded by assuring them that all things are possible with God.

But it seems obvious from this passage that the disciples themselves saw worldly wealth as a sign of God's favor. This was true even though they had heard the story of Job, in which a very wealthy man lost everything and became a pauper through no fault of his own. But Jesus knew that when we have too much, we tend to take our faith and our hope away from God and put it on our possessions.

In His parable of the rich man and Lazarus, Jesus again shocked the crowds by portraying a rich man as the villain of the story. This simply went against the current of Jewish thinking of that time.

Let me say it again: *It is crucial that we cling to God as tightly during good times as we do during bad.* It is as vital to seek Him diligently when things are going our way as it is to seek Him when everything seems to be stacked against us. Our lives are in His hands at all times. Success in this world is temporary and not at all important in the eternal scheme of things.

Abiding in Yeshua

Andrew Murray was one of the great heroes of our faith. He was a giant of a man, even though he was small in stature and weighed less than one hundred pounds. Murray was born in South Africa in 1828, earned a master's degree when he was just seventeen, and was ordained in the Dutch Reformed Church at the age of twenty. He wrote several books that are considered Christian classics, including *With Christ in the School of Prayer, Absolute Surrender,* and *The Prayer Life.* In another of his works, *Abide in Christ,* Murray wrote eloquently about the importance of following Yeshua's command to abide in Him:

> If, in our orthodox Churches, the abiding in Christ, the living union with Him, the experience of His daily and hourly presence and keeping, were preached with the same distinctness and urgency as His atonement and pardon through His blood, I am confident that many would be found to accept with gladness the invitation to such a life, and that its influence would be manifest in their experience of the purity and the power, the love and the joy, the fruit-bearing, and all the blessedness which the Saviour connected with the abiding in Him.[1]

Murray was distressed that so many believers were not living joyful, victorious lives. As author and editor William J. Petersen wrote:

The great evangelists of the nineteenth century—D. L. Moody, Charles Finney, R. A. Torrey and others—had called thousands to Jesus Christ. But as Andrew Murray talked to these new Christians and observed their conduct, he was appalled. Many of them had never had a prayer answered. Some were living no differently now than before they were converted. And some were bickering and fussing, unhappy with others and unhappy with themselves. He wrote his books with them in mind.[2]

Murray taught that "The blessings He [Yeshua] bestows...are only to be enjoyed in close fellowship with Himself."[3] He wrote that our Lord not only called us to come to Him, but also to stay with Him.

> And yet this was in very deed His object and purpose when first He called you to Himself. It was not to refresh you for a few short hours after your conversion with the joy of His love and deliverance, and then to send you forth to wander in sadness and sin. He had destined you to something better than a short-lived blessedness, to be enjoyed only in times of special earnestness and prayer, and then to pass away, as you had to return to those duties in which far the greater part of life has to be spent. No, indeed; He had prepared for you an abiding dwelling with Himself, where your whole life and every moment of it might be spent, where the work of your daily life might be done, and where all the while you might be enjoying unbroken communion with Himself.[4]

He asks:

> Who would, after seeking the King's palace, be content to stand in the door, when he is invited in to dwell in the King's presence, and share with Him in all the glory of

His royal life? Oh, let us enter in and abide, and enjoy to the full all the rich supply.[5]

And finally, I would to close this chapter with this powerful truth from Murray's pen:

He that abides in Christ the Crucified One, learns to know what it is to be crucified with Him, and in Him to be indeed dead unto sin. He that abides in Christ the Risen and Glorified One, becomes in the same way partaker of His resurrection life, and of the glory with which He has now been crowned in heaven. Unspeakable are the blessings which flow to the soul from the union with Jesus in His glorified life.

This life is a life of perfect victory and rest.[6]

Chapter 15

IT'S NEVER TOO LATE

*Then He [ADONAI] said, "I will most surely return to you in about
a year's time, surprisingly, Sarah your wife will have a son." Sarah
was listening at the entrance of the tent, which was behind Him.
Now Abraham and Sarah were old, advanced in years—Sarah had
stopped having the way of women. So Sarah laughed to herself, saying,
"After I've grown decrepit, can I have desire—and my lord so old?"
Then ADONAI said to Abraham, "Why is it that Sarah laughed,
saying, 'Can I really give birth when I am so old?' Is anything
too difficult for ADONAI? At the appointed time I will return
to you—in about a year—and Sarah will have a son."*

—**GENESIS 18:10–14**

YOU MAY FEEL that you've made a mess of your life and it's too late to start fulfilling God's plan for you.

Not so!

As the above passage of Scripture illustrates, ours is the God of second chances. Abraham and Sarah were well past child-bearing age when Sarah became pregnant with Isaac. Isaac, in turn, gave birth to Jacob, who became father of the twelve tribes of Israel. Mighty kings and princes came into the world through the line established by Abraham and Sarah—including Yeshua, our Messiah and Savior.

THE MAN WHO DENIED THE SAVIOR

When I think about people who received a chance late in life to turn things around, the Apostle Peter comes to mind. What did Peter do? He denied the Lord—three times. Just before Yeshua was arrested, Peter promised that he would never turn his back on Him, no matter what happened. "Master, I am ready to go with You even to prison and to death," he said (Luke 22:33).

But Jesus answered, "I tell you, Peter, a rooster will not crow today until you have denied three times that you know Me" (v. 34).

Of course, Peter did exactly as Jesus had prophesied, even though I'm certain he was shocked by his own lack of courage. Peter is proof that we never know how we'll respond in a time of crisis until we come face-to-face with the moment. Peter meant well. He even pulled out his sword in the Garden of Gethsemane and cut off the ear of the high priest's servant. But after that, his bravado quickly disappeared.

Three times he was asked if he was a follower of Jesus of Nazareth, and three times he denied it. Luke tells us that just as Peter was denying for the third time that he even knew who Jesus was, the rooster crowed. "And the Lord turned and looked straight at Peter. Then Peter remembered the word of the Lord, how He had told him, 'Before the rooster crows today, you will deny Me three times.' And Peter went out and wept bitterly" (vv. 61–62).

Peter had been with Jesus for three long years. He had seen the dead raised, the blind receive sight, and the sick healed. He had been blessed to hear all of the Master's teachings. He had been in position to be one of the greatest leaders in the kingdom of God. And now he had gone and blown it all. Or at least I imagine that's how he felt. How could there possibly be any excuse for what he had done?

Yeshua was killed before Peter even had a chance to tell Him how sorry he was. Only hours after Peter's denial, the Lord was crucified. With Jesus dead, Peter must have felt that he was beyond forgiveness. How could he ever go on?

Even though Peter denied three times that he even knew the Lord, it was not enough to remove him from the depth and width of God's mercy and grace. Nowhere in the Bible do we even find Peter being chastised for what he had done. After Yeshua's resurrection, He never even said anything that came close to, "I told you so." There was never any question of Peter being removed from his place of leadership among the apostles. When the first-ever gospel sermon was preached on the Day of Pentecost, Peter was chosen to deliver it. He preached the good news of the resurrection with power and conviction that day—so much so that about three thousand souls were saved.

Peter was not defined by his denial of Jesus. He didn't have to spend the rest of his life living in the shadow of that awful moment, nor did he have to explain over and over how and why it had happened. It happened, but it wasn't the defining moment of his life. Despite what Peter did, it was never too late for him to make a "comeback" in God's service, and it's never too late for you or me either. God's mercy is greater than we can imagine.

I was radically saved at age twenty, delivered not only from using drugs but from dealing drugs as well. I prayed, studied the Bible, and shared my faith—I was a new creation. Everything changed! But I made just one mistake. I continued to live with my old buddies who were not believers. My Bible study leader told me that light had no place in darkness, but I didn't do anything about the situation. The guys were my friends, and I thought I could change them over time. Even though I witnessed to them, they continued to party, listen to druggie music, and deal their drugs. Slowly, they began to drag me down.

Then one day, about four or five months after I'd become a Christian, I got a phone call from a marijuana grower in California I'd known during my drug dealing days. He was probably one of the best growers of "high-quality sinsemilla" (seedless, high potency pot) in the country. "Hey dude," he said, "I have a great crop, and I have ten pounds ready for you as promised." I had forgotten that I'd put my order in over a year before.

The battle inside me began. "Don't do it. The old man has died," the still, small voice reminded me.

"Think of all the money you'll make," I heard in my other ear. "You can tithe on it! Think of the people you can help. And don't forget the church needs money for their building program."

In the end, I decided I would do "just one last deal." So I flew to California. While I was there, I set up dinner with one of my cousins who lives in San Francisco. We went to a Chinese restaurant, and I did something I almost never do: I opened and read the fortune inside the cookie. I was shocked when I read, "Don't give up heaven for hell just to be stubborn. Admit you're wrong." It was as if God was speaking to me in an audible voice.

The Lord is so gracious. He never gives up on us. In the midst of my sin and rebellion, God was letting me know He was not giving up on me! "The Lord is not slow in keeping his promise, as some understand slowness. Instead he is patient with you, not wanting anyone to perish, but everyone to come to repentance" (2 Pet. 3:9, NIV).

I hate to admit it, but I did go through with the drug deal, and I had some hard times in my spiritual life as a result. I made a terrible mistake that caused me much grief, but when I repented, God set my feet back on the right path.

His mercy knows no bounds. When we get to heaven, I think we'll be surprised by some of the people we'll meet there. These may include notorious criminals, tyrants, shady businessmen, hedonists, atheists, and others who lived their lives in opposition to the gospel.

Now please don't tell anyone, "Jonathan Bernis believes atheists are going to go to heaven!" I don't. But I do believe it's possible for Yeshua to save someone in the very last moments of his or her life. It only takes a few seconds to say yes to the Savior and step out of darkness and into the light.

Christopher Hitchens, who died in 2011, was a staunch opponent of Christianity—and all other religions. He wrote many best-selling books attacking faith, including *God Is Not Great,* subtitled *How Religion Poisons Everything,* and *The Portable Atheist.*

Hitchens passed away after an eighteen-month battle with esophageal cancer. During this time, he was befriended by a number of prominent Christian leaders, and thousands of believers around the world began praying for his healing and salvation. An "Everybody Pray for Hitchens Day" was scheduled, although he said he was not going to take part.

Hitchens was not healed and did not accept Yeshua as his Lord and Savior.

Or did he?

Some people insist that Hitchens received God's grace in the final hours of his life. Others insist that he stayed a strong and militant atheist until the very end. I have no way of knowing the truth. If you're interested in reading more about the situation, you can find plenty of information on the Internet.

One thing I do know is that if Christopher Hitchens *did* surrender his life to Yeshua, he is with God today. If he asked Yeshua to save him, he was saved. All of the words he wrote against God were instantly forgiven. It is never too late to accept the grace God offers. And I believe that if Christopher Hitchens did receive the Lord through faith, he is spending eternity with those who spent their lives in service of God's kingdom.

THE PARABLE OF THE LABORERS

Jesus told a parable about a man who went out early in the morning and hired a number of laborers to come work in his field for a day for a denarius—which was a proper day's wage for a field hand.

As the day wore on, he went out and hired some other men to work in his vineyard, telling them that he would pay them whatever was right.

But then:

> About the eleventh hour, he went out and found others
> standing around. And he said to them, "Why have you
> been standing here idle the whole day?"
>   "Because no one hired us," they said to him.
>   He said to them, "You go into the vineyard, too."
>   —MATTHEW 20:6–7

At the end of the day, he had his foreman gather all the men
together to pay them for their day's work. Those who were hired
first thing in the morning were pleasantly surprised when they
saw that those who had only spent one hour in the vineyard
were each given a denarius. They figured that since they had
been laboring under the hot sun all day long, the landowners
would surely pay them more.

But their joy turned to disappointment when they saw
that those who were hired in the middle of the morning also
received a denarius. And disappointment turned to anger when
they too received a denarius:

> But when they received [their pay], they began to grumble
> against the master of the house, saying, "These last guys
> did one hour, and you've made them equal to us, who
> bore the burden and scorching heat of the day!"
>   But answering, he said to one of them, "Friend, I'm
> doing you no wrong. Didn't you agree with me on a
> denarius? Take what is yours and go. But I want to give
> this last guy the same as you. Am I not permitted to do
> what I want with what belongs to me? Or is your eye evil
> because I am good?"
>   —MATTHEW 20:11–15

When I think about it, it seems to me that it would only be fair if the first-century believers had it better than the rest of us in heaven. Perhaps a few extra rooms in their mansions. Quicker access to the throne of God. They should be a little happier, a little more comfortable, a little more blessed. After all, look what they went through. They were forced to fight lions in the Roman coliseum. Burned alive for their faith. Crucified. Beheaded. Drawn and quartered. It makes me shudder when I hear about some of the ways they were tortured. These are the laborers who were hired first thing in the morning and spent the entire day in hard labor.

God does not judge as we would. He doesn't give to us because we earned something or deserve anything. He gives to us because of His grace.

Writing about the parable of the laborers, Philip Yancey says:

> I do not know how to phrase this delicately, so I will just come out and say it: I'm a bit worried about the mathematical aptitude shown in the Bible. Frederick Buechner goes so far as to call it "atrocious." I know that kind of statement gets some people riled up, but the more I look the more I understand what he means.[1]

With his tongue firmly in his cheek, Yancey goes on:

> I realize that Jesus told this parable as a lesson not on employee benefits, but on God's attitude toward us. But the mathematics seem just as odd in the spiritual realm. The upstarts in this parable remind me of the thief on the cross: a good-for-nothing who barely sneaks in under the wire and yet apparently gets the same reward as someone who has lived a lifetime of devotion and piety. Tales of last-minute forgiveness have a certain winsome quality, to be sure, but such stories will hardly motivate people to

live good Christian lives. How would you feel if you were raised in an upright family, attended Christian schools, matured, and established an exemplary home in the community, only to find that some Johnny-come-lately with a deathbed confessional edges you out on Judgment Day.[2]

Consider the thieves who were crucified with Yeshua. Who knows what kind of lives they had led? Had they murdered innocent people? Were they robbers who preyed upon innocent families traveling along the road from Jerusalem to Jericho? How many lives had they ruined, and how much wreckage had they left behind? Whatever they had done, we know they had both led lives of crime, because when the unrepentant thief mocked Jesus, the other one said, "We're getting what we deserve for our actions, and rightly so—but this One has done nothing wrong" (Luke 23:41).

And yet when the thief asked, "*Yeshua*, remember me when You come into Your kingdom," our Lord replied, "Amen, I tell you, today you shall be with Me in Paradise" (vv. 42–43).

Is it really that easy? Could all that sin and selfishness be wiped away in a single moment?

The answer, obviously, is yes. Such is the grace and mercy of the God we serve.

We don't have to compare ourselves with those heroes who have been jailed, beaten, or killed because of their faith. Those of us who live in the United States should just thank God that we live in a country where we are free to worship Him as we please, and stand up for Him in the midst of whatever persecutions may come our way.

I believe that some people who have spent their entire lives fighting against God and His kingdom have had a change of heart just before they died. And, like one of the thieves who was crucified with Jesus, they are welcomed into paradise. They too will be rewarded as if they spent their lives on the mission field.

I don't understand it. But I know that God is loving and generous, and I accept it. He says it's never too late to receive a fresh start, and I believe Him.

THE STORY OF HOWARD STORM

In my book *A Rabbi Looks at the Afterlife* I told the story of a man named Howard Storm, who says that God's grace extends further than most of us know. Howard's story is remarkable, but absolutely convincing when you hear it.

He was in Paris when he suddenly suffered a severe perforation of his duodenum. "It was the most intense pain I'd ever experienced, right in the center of my belly," he said.

A doctor arrived and announced that Howard had to have emergency surgery right away. He was rushed to the surgical center by ambulance and then, apparently, forgotten. "They put me in a room and left me there for ten hours: no doctor, no nurse, no medical attention at all. It was the weekend, and most of the staff was gone." Howard is convinced he died while in that room.

What happened was that Howard passed out due to the pain. "I don't know how long I was unconscious, but when I finally woke up, the pain was gone. My first emotion was joy: somehow, miraculously, I had gotten better. I looked around and found myself standing next to the bed, and to my confusion and horror there was something in the bed that looked exactly like my body. Somehow I knew it was really was me, but at the same time I knew I wasn't alive anymore. I can't emphasize how terrifying that realization was. This couldn't be happening.

"I heard people's voices calling my name. I went to the doorway and looked down the hallway. There were people standing there, shadowy and gray, and they were saying 'Howard, hurry, come with us. We can't wait any longer.' And I replied, 'I'm sick, I need a doctor. I need surgery.' And they were saying, 'We don't have time for this. We know all about you. We've been waiting a long time for you.'"

Howard followed the voices down the hall, but he quickly sensed that he was in danger. "I knew that, wherever I was, I was not in Paris, I was not in the hospital, and I wasn't going to surgery. At that point I understood something bad was happening. I finally told them I wasn't going with them any further. The only problem was, I had no idea where I actually was. I was surrounded by complete, abject darkness, and I didn't know which way to go. And the dark shadowy figures all around me insisted, 'You're almost there.'"

They began pushing and pulling him, calling him names and hitting him.

"I fought back as best I could," Howard said. "That only made them more violent and vicious, biting, scratching, and tearing at me. The way I thought about it was that I had been flushed down the sewage system into the cesspool of the universe. The worst thing was that, deep down inside, I knew I belonged there. I had no excuse for the way I had lived my life. Now I was dead and this was my fate."

Suddenly Howard heard a voice command, "Pray to God."

"But I don't believe in God."

"Pray to God."

"But I don't know how to pray."

He remembered a few words from The Lord's Prayer and the 23rd Psalm. "All I could recall were bits and pieces. As I began to mutter these things, trying my best to remember, the people around me became very, very agitated and angry and telling me that there was no God, that nobody could hear me, and that now they were going to make it much worse for me than what they'd already done.

"But I noticed that when I mentioned God, it drove them away. It was as if they couldn't stand being in the presence of that name. It finally drove them away completely, and I was left alone to think about my life. An incalculable amount of time passed, as I considered everything I had done and said and thought. And I realized that my life was devoid of anything except my own selfish desires and that the people who had brought me to this place had been ruled by the same self-serving ends.

"My life, I now understood, was absent of love, absent of light, absent of hope, absent of all good things. It was, in short, utter darkness. I was just like them: ripping and tearing and biting and trying to dominate others. I was one of them. I had the veneer of being a nice guy, a respected college professor and all that, but in my heart was just my own neediness."

Suddenly He remembered singing "Jesus Loves Me" as a child. "Not only did I remember the words, but I remembered as a child believing in something other than myself."

Howard Storm called out to Jesus, "Please save me."

"And He came to me then, and reached down in the darkness, bathed in brilliant white light which allowed me to finally see myself as I was, nothing but a mass of blood and gore from what had been done to me. He reached down and touched me, and all my wounds disappeared and I was made whole. But more importantly, He filled me with a love that I can't possibly begin to describe. There are no words adequate to express His love for us and His love, specifically, for me in that moment.

"With that, He picked me up and put His arms around me and held me very tight against Him and stroked my back as I cried and wept for joy. I realized that, not only did He love me—not in some kind of condescending way—but that He really *liked* me as a friend. It was, in fact, as if I'd found the best friend I'd ever known. He really knew me, more than my parents, more than my wife; He really *knew* me."

Howard told me, "The Bible says in four different places that anyone who calls upon the name of the Lord will be saved. I had called out His name and He had answered me."

Today, as I said, Howard Storm is fulfilling his calling as a minister of the gospel. If it was not too late for him, then it's certainly not too late for you or me. God's grace is bigger and stronger than any sins we may have committed or failures we may have experienced.

A Failure Named Lincoln

Whenever I think about someone who overcame years of failure to achieve great success, my mind turns to Abraham Lincoln.

If you asked one hundred Americans to name the best president the United States has ever had, I'm pretty sure that at least half of them would name Lincoln. But for most of his life, it certainly didn't look like that was going to be the case. You may know the story.

As a young man, Lincoln twice failed in business. Then he suffered through a personal tragedy, when a young woman he loved and wanted to marry fell sick and died. Surely that was enough tragedy for anyone to take; but life wasn't about to ease up on Lincoln.

He lost his first attempt to win a seat in the Illinois state legislature. Then he tried twice to win a spot in the US House of Representatives, and lost both times. After that, he turned his attention to the Senate, where he endured two more defeats.

He was nominated for vice president, but again lost, and suffered through the illness and death of a beloved son. Then, after he was elected president of the United States, the country was torn apart by civil war. After presiding over four years of the bloodiest war in American history, he was assassinated.

For the most part, his life sounds like one disaster after another. And yet Abraham Lincoln was used by God to make the world a better place for everyone. He, more than any other human being, was responsible for ending slavery in the United States and bringing about true equality between human beings. And, like the Apostle Paul, I am convinced he can say that the sufferings he endured during his lifetime are as nothing compared to the blessings that will be his for all eternity. We human beings have a very limited perspective. But God doesn't. He sees the whole picture, and we can always know that He desires what is absolutely best for us.

Chapter 16

HIS BLESSINGS ARE ALL AROUND US

The heavens declare the glory of God,
and the sky shows His handiwork.

—PSALM 19:2

I BELIEVE WE MISS many of God's greatest blessings simply because we don't open our eyes and look for them. They're all around us, but we don't see them.

Many times, God speaks through the situations and circumstances He brings into our lives. But we'll never know it if we don't keep our eyes and ears open.

Yeshua said that the kingdom of heaven is like a tiny seed that grows up to become the greatest of all trees. I believe this is a principle that transcends all areas of life. Good things—big things—sometimes come in small and seemingly insignificant packages, like the peanut. We have to open our eyes and see them.

Think about what a blessing it is to live in the United States. In my role with Jewish Voice, I spend a great deal of time on airplanes, and I travel to some of the world's poorest countries and areas.

Every time I get back from one of those trips, I am so grateful for the comforts of life here in the States. I can flip a switch and light fills the room. I turn the tap and water pours out. I can take a shower anytime I want, and I have a nice, warm bed to sleep in. I have a closet full of clothes and a refrigerator full of food. We truly are the most blessed people in the history of the world.

And yet, sadly, after a few days at home, I start to forget about how rough it was out there in the field. I take it for granted that the electricity, water, food, and other "necessities" of life will be available to me at the flip of a switch or the push of a button.

As I said, it's easy to overlook our blessings.

Sometimes it seems that the more blessings we have, the easier it is to forget to be thankful. One of the things Jewish

Voice does on a regular basis is take medical care to impoverished Jews in Ethiopia. As you already know, Ethiopia is one of the poorest countries in the world. Millions of people there don't have adequate food, healthcare, or shelter. And in general, Ethiopia's thousands of Jews are the poorest of the poor.

They face discrimination and hardship simply because they are Jews. Many thousands are waiting to make *aliyah*—that is, go home—to Israel. But for now they are stuck in Ethiopia, because terrorism and attacks from Israel's neighbors have had a severe negative impact on the country's economy. Israel can't afford a massive influx of people when there are few jobs and other opportunities for them.

My purpose is not to discuss the economic situation in Israel, but rather to talk about what happens when we provide medical care for these gentle Ethiopian Jews. You should see the grateful tears rolling down their faces and the big smiles when they discover that we've come there to help them. Even the smallest thing we do for them brings on a torrent of gratitude and blessing. They simply can't thank us enough for what we do for them and their children. They don't have as many blessings as we do, but they savor every one they do have.

The seventeenth chapter of Luke tells of an occasion when Jesus healed ten men who were suffering from leprosy (vv. 11–19). The Bible says the men stood at a distance and begged Jesus to have mercy on them. He told them to go show themselves to the priest, and as they were on their way, they were all healed. One of the men came back, "praising God in a loud voice. He threw himself at Jesus' feet and thanked him—and he was a Samaritan" (v. 15, NIV).

Where did the other nine go? We don't know. They got their healing and then went on their way. Jesus said, "Were not all ten cleansed? Where are the other nine?" (v. 17, NIV). Have you ever been one of the ungrateful nine? I admit that I have. But I will make every effort to see that it doesn't happen again.

THE GOD OF SECOND, THIRD, AND FOURTH CHANCES

But whenever we are ungrateful, or miss the mark in other ways, we have a God who is always ready to forgive us and give us a fresh start, no matter how often we mess up. As long as we ask Him sincerely, He will forgive. This doesn't mean we can go on doing things that we know are wrong because "God is always ready to forgive." Sincerity is the key. We must sincerely repent, or turn away, from wrong behaviors and attitudes.

I'm sure you've heard of George Foreman, the former heavyweight boxing champion who became even more famous selling his George Foreman grill on television. Foreman admits that when he was a boy he was a bully with a chip on his shoulder. That rage stayed with him as he became one of the most successful and most feared boxers of all time. Then God got hold of him. Suddenly, George Foreman was filled with joy and peace. He became known as a gentle teddy bear of a man. He was rarely without a big smile on his face or an encouraging word on his lips.

He still continued to use the athletic skills God had given him, but he was no longer cruel or vicious. He started a church and became a pastor. He used much of his time in the spotlight to talk about God's love. Seventeen years after becoming a believer, George Foreman recaptured boxing's heavyweight title at the age of forty-five, becoming the oldest ever to win the crown.

It is never too late for God to do something special in someone's life.

The Book of Matthew tells of an occasion when Peter came to Jesus and asked, "Lord, how many times shall I forgive my brother or sister who sins against me? Up to seven times?"

Jesus answered, "I tell you, not seven times, but seventy-seven times" (Matt. 18:21–22, NIV).

Of course, the seventy-seven is symbolic. Seven is God's perfect number, so when Jesus says we must forgive seventy-seven times, He is really saying that we must be ready to forgive an infinite number of offenses. This is a mirror of the way God treats us.

As often as we fall, He is there to pick us up and put our feet back on the right path.

Even as He suffered and died on the cross, Jesus prayed, "Father, forgive them, for they do not know what they are doing" (Luke 23:34).

What makes that even more amazing to me is that I know Yeshua had the power to come down from the cross and wreak havoc on His enemies. He could have proved to them that He was exactly who He said He was—the Messiah, the Son of God. And He could have destroyed them with a single look. But He didn't do it. What amazing love and restraint He showed—something I know I never could have done. It's hard enough for me to overlook the smallest slight. What about you? How we need to be more like our God, whose mercy knows no bounds.

Every time I read through the Bible, I'm amazed at God's willingness to forgive those who doubt Him, find fault with Him, and refuse to obey His commands. There are many examples of this in the Bible's account of the Israelites' journey out of Egypt.

Chapter 14 of Exodus tells us that when the Israelites saw that the Egyptians were pursuing them, they cried out, "Have you taken us away to die in the wilderness because there were no graves in Egypt? Why have you dealt this way with us, to bring us out of Egypt? Did we not say to you in Egypt, 'Let us alone, so that we may serve the Egyptians?' It was better for us to serve the Egyptians than to die in the wilderness!" (vv. 11–12).

Despite their disbelief and their complaining, God fought for them, and the Egyptians were drowned in the Red Sea.

Yet only two chapters later, Exodus 16:3 tells us that on the fifteenth day of the second month after the Israelites came out of Egypt, they complained, "If only we had died by the hand of ADONAI in the land of Egypt, when we sat by pots of meat, when we ate bread until we were full. But you have brought us into the wilderness, to kill this entire congregation with hunger."

God responded to the grumbling by raining down bread from heaven.

But in the very next chapter, the Israelites are up to their old tricks. "Why have you brought us up out of Egypt? To kill us with thirst, along with our children and cattle?" (Exod. 17:3).

This time God gave them water from a rock.

A few chapters later, when Moses was up on Mount Sinai, getting God's laws for the people, they melted down all their jewelry, formed a golden calf, and began worshipping it as the God who brought them out of Egypt.

And not long after that they were complaining about the manna. "The grumblers among them began to have cravings, so *Bnei-Yisrael* began to wail repeatedly, saying, 'If we could just eat some meat! We remember the fish that we used to eat in Egypt, for free—the cucumbers, the melons, the leeks, the onions, and the garlic! But now we have no appetite. We never see anything but this manna'" (Num. 11:4–6).

Read through the rest of the Old Testament and you'll see that this pattern continued throughout the history of Israel. Despite all the signs and wonders God performed for them, the Israelites turned away and worshipped idols. It got so bad during the time of the prophet Elijah that he thought he was the only one living for God. In the eighteenth chapter of 1 Kings, Elijah says that he is the only one of the Lord's prophets left in Israel. But Baal, the Canaanite god, is represented by four hundred fifty prophets who eat at the king's table, and an additional four hundred prophets of Asherah. What a sorry state of affairs. And yet God refused to abandon them to their sinful ways.

Because the wicked queen, Jezebel, wanted to kill him, Elijah fled into the wilderness. First Kings 19:13–18 tells of the prophet's encounter with God:

> Then all of a sudden, a voice addressed him and said, "What are you doing here, Elijah?"
>
> "I have been very zealous for ADONAI *Tzva'ot,*" he said, "for the children of Israel have forsaken Your covenant, torn down Your altars, and slain Your prophets with the sword—and I alone am left, and they are seeking to take my life!" Then ADONAI said to him, "Go, return on your way to the wilderness of Damascus, and when you get there, anoint Hazael king over Aram, and anoint Jehu son of Nimshi king over Israel, and anoint Elisha son of Shaphat of Abel-meholah as prophet in your place. It shall come to pass that whoever escapes from the sword of Hazael, Jehu will slay; and whoever escapes from the sword of Jehu, Elisha will slay. Yet I have preserved seven

thousand in Israel whose knees have not bowed to Baal and whose mouth has not kissed him."

Elijah was mistaken to think that he was the only person in Israel who hadn't bowed down to Baal. But he hadn't missed by much. Only seven thousand people in the entire nation were loyal to Yahweh, the only true God, who had created the heavens and earth and brought the Israelites out of slavery in Egypt. It's hard to imagine, but the descendants of Abraham, Isaac, and Jacob turned against the one true God, Creator of the universe, and began worshipping the impotent, capricious weather gods of their Canaanite neighbors. Sun gods, moon gods, rain gods, and so on.

I remember many times when God has blessed me in amazing ways. He has protected me in times of danger. He's given me guidance when I didn't know which way to turn. I have experienced His healing touch. He has given me the privilege and thrill of sharing His love as a Messianic rabbi.

As you look back over your own life, you may see many ways God has blessed you. Don't let go of them or forget about them. You might remember the old song that reminds us to count our many blessings. You may even want to write them down and keep them somewhere close at hand where you can get them out and read them from time to time.

When God sent Moses to confront Pharaoh, He told him:

> Go to Pharaoh, because I have hardened his heart and the heart of his servants, so that I might show these My signs in their midst, and so you may tell your son and your grandchildren what I have done in Egypt, as well as My signs that I did among them, so you may know that I am ADONAI.
>
> —EXODUS 10:1–2

God expects us to remember all the ways He has blessed us, and to share the stories of those victories with our families and friends. When we do this, His name will be exalted and our own faith will be deepened. When we recall how God has delivered and blessed us in the past, it's easier to believe that He can and will do it again.

If your walk of faith is relatively new, keep your eyes open and look for the ways God is blessing you. I'm convinced that most of us experience miracles every day, but we miss most of them because we don't have our eyes open wide enough. Whenever God does something special for you, write it down so you won't forget about it.

I know a man who has been in ministry for at least twenty-five years. When he was just starting out, struggling as the "low man on the totem pole" in a large church, a visiting pastor gave him an especially encouraging prophecy about all the ways God was going to use him in his ministry.

Because the service was recorded, he was later able to get a transcript of that prophecy, which he folded up and put in his billfold. He has carried those encouraging words with him every day since then. He says that he's taken that paper out at least one hundred times and read those precious words. He reads them when he's tired. He reads them when he's discouraged. He reads them when things are going great and he's tempted to think that his success is of his own making. They remind him what God thinks of him and help him stay focused on what's really important. Yes, after all these years, the paper is wrinkled and torn, but even that helps him remember that God is the same yesterday, today, and forever.

Never forget that God is always there for you, and He loves you more than you can imagine.

A Man Named Luckey

Let me tell you about a man by the name of Jack Luckey.[1] Jack was born into a committed Christian family. They were in church every time the doors were open. He accepted Jesus as His Lord and Savior at a very young age, and he learned the Bible. But as Jack entered his teen years, he began to have doubts about his faith. It all seemed too easy, too simplistic. Eventually he left behind everything that had to do with his Christian upbringing. He stopped reading the Bible. He never prayed. He became a staunch atheist.

As is befitting a man with the last name of Luckey, that's not where his story ends.

He married a woman named Camilla who, like him, considered herself an atheist. But somewhere along the line, things changed for her. She started going to church, reading her Bible—and for two years, she prayed that her husband would turn back to God.

Jack wasn't happy about any of this. But he prided himself on the fact that he wasn't a controlling man. If Camilla wanted to believe in God, that was her business. But it wasn't something he wanted. He sometimes challenged her by saying, "If there really were a God, don't you think He would _____?" Try as he might, he couldn't seem to get through to her.

Despite his antagonism toward his wife's faith, he went with Camilla every Sunday to the little Episcopal church where her life had been changed. When his wife walked forward to take Communion, he always went with her. But just before they reached the altar, he would slip out a side door and spend a few minutes smoking a cigarette.

Then, one Saturday morning, Camilla couldn't find her Bible. She looked all around the house but just couldn't remember where she had last been reading it.

After helping his wife look for her precious Bible, Jack wandered out into their backyard. "If there really were a God," he thought, "and He really cared for Camilla, He'd show her where that Bible is." Adding an exclamation point to his inner dialogue, he kicked at a plastic bucket, sending it flipping across the grass. As it tumbled, something fell out.

His wife's Bible!

What in the world was that Bible doing in a bucket in the backyard?

On Sunday, Jack went to church with Camilla, as usual. But all during the service, he kept thinking about that Bible in the bucket. When the congregation was called to receive Communion, he walked forward with his wife. But this time he wasn't sure if he should slip out the side door for a smoke. He didn't really know why, but he felt that maybe he should stay. In this state of confusion, he silently threw up another challenge. He thought of the hymn he had often heard when he was a boy, "Just As I Am." He had sung that song hundreds of times, usually as part of the altar call. But you didn't hear old camp meeting songs like that one in the Episcopal Church.

"If there really is a God," He said to himself, "He should have them sing, 'Just As I Am.' Then I'll stay and take Communion."

Imagine his shock when the little orchestra immediately launched into the old hymn. At that instant, he heard the still, small voice of the Spirit whispering to him, "Jack, you know I'm here. Now what are you going to do about it? You can turn left and leave by the side door and I will leave you alone, or you can turn right to the Communion rail and come to me."

Of course, Jack took a right turn and took Communion for the first time in many years.

But just in case that wasn't enough to convince him that God cared about him and was with him, the Lord had one more amazing thing to show him.

Jack always rode his bicycle to work, even though he had to go through heavy traffic to reach his office in Washington DC. It so happened that the very next day after "the miracle" at church was the first Monday after daylight savings time ended, which meant that it would get darker much earlier. That was OK, because Jack had a light on his bike to help him navigate through traffic at night. The problem was that he hadn't needed the light at all for the past few months, and he had forgotten to check to make sure it was working. It was already dark when he came out of his office at the end of the day—and the light *wasn't* working.

He knew it wouldn't be safe to ride home without a light on his bike, but what else could he do? Almost instinctively he thought, "God, if You really loved me, You'd give me light." He flipped the light switch again, and it came on immediately—and it stayed on all the way home.

But as soon as he pulled into his driveway, the light blinked out and would not come on again. That's when a startling thought hit Jack. The light drew its power from a generator, but Jack had been intending to do some maintenance on that generator a few months earlier. He had removed some essential parts, planning to go back and replace them later on—but he had forgotten to do it. There was no way the generator could work without those parts. Thus, there was no way the light could have shined—and yet it had. Once again God had shown His love for someone who had turned his back on Him.

Looking back on those amazing incidents, Jack Luckey says, "Here was the God of the universe, who took the time to show me he was there, even when I was such a stubborn jerk."[2]

Chapter 17

WALK IN BLESSING

I am with you always, even to the end of the age.

—MATTHEW 28:20

WHAT A WONDERFUL thing it is to know that we have a heavenly Father who loves us, cares about what we are going through, and promises to prosper us and give us hope and a future. I've discovered that when you really believe God's promise, you can handle just about anything the devil or this world can throw at you. I've also discovered that God means exactly what He says. The more we trust Him, the more He blesses.

Even when something bad happens, we can have more peace about it because we know that God is in charge, and that it's all part of His plan. As Philippians 4:6–7 says, "Do not be anxious about anything—but in everything, by prayer and petition with thanksgiving, let your requests be made known to God. And the *shalom* of God, which surpasses all understanding, will guard your hearts and your minds in Messiah *Yeshua*."

My purpose in writing this book has been to let you know that God desires the very best for you. He loves you more than you can possibly understand. If He had a refrigerator, your photo would be stuck there in a magnetic photo frame. His wallet would be full of photos of you, and He would be the type to pull them out and bore strangers by going on and on about how wonderful you are. I don't mean to be flippant. But these are two of the best ways I can think of to illustrate how much He loves you.

Here's a third and even more important way to measure the depth of His love: He sent His Son to die for you.

But as we have seen, He is not an indulgent Father who wants us to have an easy time of it. He wants all of us to fulfill the potential He gave us. And He is there to walk with us every step of the way as we strive to become the best men and women we can possibly be.

I want to spend the remainder of our time together touching on some of what we've discussed in the pages of this book:

God is still on His throne.

This world can be an uncertain, confusing, and dangerous place, but God has everything under control, and He has a plan for your life. He says, "For I know the plans I have for you…plans to prosper you and not to harm you, plans to give you hope and a future" (Jer. 29:11, NIV). When I say that God is in control, does this mean He has caused things like terrorist bombings, crime, natural disasters, and outbreaks of disease? Not at all. We live in a fallen world, and evil forces are at work here. But in the end, everything will work out just as God has planned, and evil will be swept away forever.

God is with His people even during times of captivity.

When God gave the promise that is recorded in Jeremiah 29:11, His people were being held captive in Babylon. Most of us are held captive by something: Sin. Painful memories. Fear. Doubt. Whatever it is that holds you captive, you can be sure that God is there with you, and for you, and wants to help you obtain your freedom.

God has not forgotten you.

Satan is lying to you when he tells you that you are insignificant, or that you are already condemned because of sins you have committed. God not only knows you by name, He knows how many hairs you have on your head. You are an important part of His plan for this world, and He is always ready to forgive you and cleanse you of all unrighteousness when you ask Him sincerely and turn away from sinful behavior.

God desires to give you shalom.

Although this Hebrew word is often translated as "peace," it is really much more. Shalom is a sense of wellness, happiness, welfare, prosperity, completeness, health, rest, safety, and wholeness. In Jeremiah 29:11, God is telling us that He wants us to walk in health, safety, peace, and divine rest. As Yeshua says in Matthew 11:28–30, "Come to Me, all who are weary and burdened, and I will give you rest. Take My yoke upon you and learn from Me, for I am gentle and humble in heart, and 'you will find rest for your souls.' For My yoke is easy and My burden is light."

God expects obedience.

God does not exist to serve us. It's the other way around. He is the One who gave us life and created everything we see. How could we not fear Him and treat Him with the reverence and respect He deserves? Yet some people today have come to view Him as an indulgent, doting Grandfather who looks the other way when people engage in selfish, sinful behavior—or who simply smiles and says, "Kids will be kids." As I've said again and again, He is always ready to forgive us when we fall short. But He does expect us to strive to be obedient. Acts 17:30–31 says that God "commands everyone everywhere to repent. For He has set a day on which He will judge the world in righteousness, through a Man whom He has appointed. He has brought forth evidence of this to all men, by raising Him from the dead."

God sees great potential in you.

If you lack confidence in yourself, you must learn to see yourself as He does. God does not judge you on the basis of what you have done, where you've been, or how much money you have in your bank account. He's not disappointed in you because you haven't yet been promoted to vice president, or because you don't drive a Mercedes. (On the other hand, He doesn't think any more of you because you *have* been promoted to vice president or *do* drive a Mercedes.) God looks into your heart. He sees you the way you want to be, rather than the way you are. He sees potential in you that you don't even know is there. The Bible says in Psalm 139:14 (NIV) that you are "fearfully and wonderfully made," and you are. Plus, if you have surrendered yourself to Yeshua, He sees you as perfectly righteous.

If you go through the fire, Yeshua will meet you there. I suppose I should not say "if" but "when." We all spend time in the fire at one time or another, even though God is blessing us. In fact, going through tough times can be a blessing, for two reasons: First, because it refines our faith and builds spiritual strength in us. Second, and most important, it is in the midst of the fire that we find the Son of God walking with us, putting His arms around us, and keeping us from being consumed by the flames.

James 1:2–4 says, "Consider it all joy, my brethren, when you encounter various trials, knowing that the testing of your faith produces endurance. And let endurance have its perfect work, so that you may be perfect and complete, lacking in nothing."

You can always trust God's timing.

Everything may not happen exactly when we want it to happen. Most of us are impatient. Because we don't see things from God's perspective, we tend to think things are moving much too slowly. Relax! God has a plan, He knows best, and His timing is perfect. On the other side of the coin, if God says, "Move now," He means it!

Yeshua said that God will bless us when we "seek first" His kingdom and His righteousness (Matt. 6:33). As I said in chapter 9, He is not obligated to bless people who never give Him a second thought. He expects to be our top priority, and if He is, then we will certainly want to spend time with Him in prayer, meditation, reading His Word, and fellowshipping with other believers.

All of these things are important, but I also want to say a few words about the importance of finding and joining a Bible-believing church in your community. When Christian pollster George Barna asked the American people what helps them grow in their faith, church attendance did not even make the top ten. The Barna Group says:

> Although church involvement was once a cornerstone of American life, U.S. adults today are evenly divided on the importance of attending church. While half (49 percent) say it is "somewhat" or "very" important, the other 51 percent say it is "not too" or "not at all" important… Looking to future generations does not paint an optimistic picture for the importance of churchgoing. Millennials (those thirty and under) stand out as least likely to value church attendance; only two in ten believe it is important. And more than one-third of Millennial young adults (35 percent) take an anti-church stance.[1]

Barna says that church attendance in the United States has declined over the last decade, with about 40 percent of the population attending services each week. This is a disheartening trend, because meeting together with other believers is one of the most important ways we grow strong in our faith. The writer of Hebrews says, "Let us hold unswervingly to the hope we profess, for he who promised is faithful. And let us consider how we may spur one another on toward love and good deeds, not giving up meeting together, as some are in the habit of doing, but encouraging one another—and all the more as you see the Day approaching" (Heb. 10:23–25, NIV).

If your plan for yourself doesn't line up with God's plan for you, change your plan.

My plan was to get a degree in business and become a millionaire by the time I was thirty. God's plan for me was to go into ministry and to allow Him to work through me to reach the Jewish people with the good news that our Messiah is on His throne in heaven and will soon be coming back to rule in Jerusalem. I am so glad I'm following His plan and not mine. Even if you don't understand it at first, following God's plan for you will bring you peace of mind and fill your heart with joy.

We must not forget God when times are good.

Some people become devoted believers when times are tough and their backs are against the wall. They pray, study their Bibles, and you'll see them in church. But when things begin to turn around, faith gives way to self-confidence. They put God on the back-burner and forget how He helped them.

You may have heard the old joke about the man whose house was inundated by floodwaters. As the water rose higher and higher, he sat on the roof pleading, "God, please help me! Please, God, please!" Just as he finished praying, a man in a boat came rowing toward him, calling out, "Hang on! I'll be right there to pick you up." The fellow looked up to heaven and said, "Never mind, God. I'll go with this guy in the rowboat." God sends rowboat after rowboat, and some folks never realize it.

Some say that one of the worst days for the Christian faith was the day Constantine the Great declared Christianity to be the state religion. Something vital was lost on that day. It was no longer risky to be a Christian. In fact, it was the easy thing to do. This led to a watering-down of the truth, and the church began to drift away from the Rock upon which it was founded.

We must guard our hearts when times are good, and not let our own "success" blind us to His constant grace and mercy.

It's never too late to come to God and start living in the flow of His blessings.

The thief on the cross did it in the very last hours of his life. I have seen people turn to God as they lay on their deathbeds. I have also seen lifetime criminals changed by Yeshua's love. Men who were thought of as coldhearted and vicious were changed by their Savior's love and welcomed into His kingdom.

With God, it's never three strikes and you're out. As long as you are living, He is standing there with open arms, ready to welcome you home. In fact, He is pursuing you, in the same way the father ran to meet the prodigal son.

It doesn't matter what you've done or where you've been. God is ready and willing to forgive and forget. His promise of hope and a future goes out to all who have accepted the salvation He offers.

Thank you for the time we've spent together in this book.

I hope my words have encouraged you, deepened your faith in God, and given you hope for tomorrow. Never forget that God is on your side. And when God is with you, there is nothing you can't do.

NOTES

CHAPTER 1
GOD HAS A PLAN FOR YOU

1. David M. Schwartz, *How Much Is a Million?* (New York: Lothrop, Lee & Shepherd Books, 1985), 19.
2. "Did You Know This? Surprising Tidbits on Hair," Schwarzkopf, accessed September 24, 2015, http://www.schwarzkopf .international/sk/en/home/hair_repair/tips_and_tricks/hair _science/amazing_titbits_on_hair.html.

CHAPTER 2
WHAT HOLDS YOU CAPTIVE?

1. Lenya Heitzig, *Holy Moments: Recognizing God's Fingerprints in Your Life* (Grand Rapids, MI: Fleming H. Revell, 2006); George H. Edeal, "Why the Choir Was Late," *LIFE*, March 27, 1950, 19–23.
2. Eugene H. Peterson, *Run With the Horses* (Downers Grove, IL: InterVarsity Press, 1983), 147–148.
3. Ibid., 154–155.
4. "Drowning Facts and Figures," International Life Saving Federation, accessed September 24, 2015, http://ilsf.org/content /drowning-facts-and-figures.
5. George MacDonald, as quoted in *The HCSB Student Bible* (Nashville: B&H Publishing Group, 2007), 802.

CHAPTER 3
WHY DO WE STRUGGLE TO
BELIEVE GOD'S PROMISES?

1. Brennan Manning, *The Furious Longing of God* (Colorado Springs, CO: David C. Cook, 2009), 36.

2. Thomas A. Tarrants, *The Conversion of a Klansman: The Story of a Former Ku Klux Klan Terrorist* (New York: Doubleday, 1979), Foreword.

3. C. S. Lewis, *The Joyful Christian* (New York: Simon & Schuster, 1996), 7.

4. John Sherrill, *They Speak With Other Tongues* (Grand Rapids, MI; Baker Books, 2004), 54.

5. Ibid., 54–56.

6. Brennan Manning, *Abba's Child* (Carol Stream, IL: Tyndale, 2015), 3.

7. Ibid., 5.

CHAPTER 4
UNDERSTANDING GOD'S PLAN FOR YOUR LIFE

1. Philip Yancey, *Soul Survivor* (Colorado Springs, CO: WaterBrook Press, 2001), 3.

CHAPTER 5
GOD'S PLANS TO PROSPER YOU

1. Cornelius Plantinga, *Engaging God's World* (Grand Rapids, MI: Eerdman's, 2003), 14–15.

CHAPTER 6
GOD WILL KEEP YOU FROM HARM

1. "The Jewish Temples: The Babylonian Exile," Jewish Virtual Library, accessed January 19, 2016, http://www.jewishvirtual library.org/jsource/History/Exile.html.

2. Terry McGonigal, "'If You Only Knew What Would Bring Peace': Shalom Theology as the Biblical Foundation for Diversity"; published online at http://studentlife.biola.edu/page _attachments/0000/1395/ShalomTheology-TerryMcGonigal.pdf.

3. Ibid.

4. Ibid.

5. Ibid.

6. Bryant L. Myers, *Walking With the Poor* (Maryknoll, NY: Orbis, 2011) 82.

CHAPTER 8
GOD WILL GIVE YOU A GLORIOUS FUTURE

1. Taken from *Encyclopedia Britannica*, 1952, paragraph 620, p. 285; see also "Seven Wonders of Jewish History," SimpleToRemember.com, accessed January 18, 2016, http://www.simpleto remember.com/articles/a/7-wonders-of-jewish-history/.
2. Walker Percy, *The Message in the Bottle* (New York: Farrar, Straus and Giroux, 1954), 6.
3. Calvin Miller, *Into the Depths of God* (Minneapolis, MN: Bethany House Publishers, 2000), 131.
4. Jonathan Bernis, *A Rabbi Looks at the Last Days* (Grand Rapids, MI: Chosen Books, 2013). Reprinted with permission.
5. Mark Twain, "Concerning the Jews," *Harper's Magazine*, September 1899, viewed January 18, 2016, at Ohr Somayach, http://ohr.edu/judaism/concern/concerna.htm.
6. Leo Tolstoy, *What Is the Jew?* printed in Jewish World periodical, 1908.
7. William J. Petersen and Randy Petersen, *100 Amazing Answers to Prayer* (Grand Rapids, MI: Fleming H. Revell, 2003), 41–42.
8. Ibid.
9. Ibid.

CHAPTER 9
SEEK FIRST HIS KINGDOM

1. Brennan Manning, *The Ragamuffin Gospel* (Sisters, OR: Multnomah Publishers, 1990), 115–116.
2. C. J. Jung, *Modern Man in Search of a Soul* (New York: Harcourt, Brace and World Harvest Books, 1933), 235.
3. Henri J. M. Nouwen, *Life of the Beloved* (New York: Crossway, 1992), 21.
4. "Jim Elliot Quote," Billy Graham Center Archives, accessed September 26, 2015, http://www2.wheaton.edu/bgc/archives/faq/20.htm.
5. Jonathan Bernis, *A Rabbi Looks at Jesus of Nazareth* (Grand Rapids, MI: Chosen Books, 2011). Reprinted with permission.

Chapter 10
Learn to See Yourself Through God's Eyes

1. Daniel Goleman, *Emotional Intelligence* (New York: Bantam, 1995).
2. Alan Loy McGinnis, *The Power of Optimism* (New York: Harper Collins, 1990), 100; Robert Schuller, In Search of Morality (Grand Rapids, MI: F. H. Revell, 1997).
3. Ibid.
4. As quoted in Bulent Atalay and Keith Wamsley, *Leonardo's Universe: The Renaissance World of Leonardo Da Vinci* (N.p.: National Geographic, 2009), 277.
5. "Who Was Alfred Adler?" North American Society of Adlerian Psychology, accessed September 26, 2015, http://www.alfred adler.org/alfred-adler.

Chapter 11
Walk in Obedience

1. "Am I a Soldier of the Cross?" by Isaac Watts, 1721. Public domain.
2. Petersen and Petersen, *100 Amazing Answers to Prayer.*
3. Ibid.
4. Ibid., 179–180.

Chapter 12
God Is Always on Time

1. Miller, *Into the Depths of God,* 35.
2. Ibid., 49.
3. Ibid., 48.
4. Mark Twain, *Roughing It,* vol. 2 (New York: Harper and Brothers Publishers, 1913), 253–254.
5. Ibid., 285.
6. Michael Brown, *Answering Jewish Objections to Jesus* (Grand Rapids, MI: Baker Books, 2000), 70.
7. Ibid., 70–71.
8. Petersen and Petersen, *100 Amazing Answers to Prayer,* 129.
9. Ibid., 130.
10. Ibid., 129–130
11. Peterson, *Run With the Horses,* 152–153.

CHAPTER 14
DON'T FORGET GOD WHEN ALL IS WELL

1. Andrew Murray, *Abide in Christ* (New Canaan, CT: Keats Publishing, 1973), Preface, v–vi.
2. Ibid., Introduction, xi–xii.
3. Ibid., 1.
4. Ibid., 2.
5. Ibid., 3.
6. Ibid., 156.

CHAPTER 15
IT'S NEVER TOO LATE

1. Philip Yancey, *I Was Just Wondering* (Grand Rapids, MI: William B. Eerdman's Publishing, 1998), 206.
2. Ibid., 207.

CHAPTER 16
HIS BLESSINGS ARE ALL AROUND US

1. Petersen and Petersen, *100 Amazing Answers to Prayer*, 132–134.
2. Ibid, 134.

CHAPTER 17
WALK IN BLESSING

1. "Americans Divided on the Importance of Church," Barna Group, March 24, 2014, https://www.barna.org/barna-update/culture/661-americans-divided-on-the-importance-of-church#.Vpzm2em0PIU.

CONNECT WITH US!

CHARISMA HOUSE

(Spiritual Growth)

Facebook.com/CharismaHouse

@CharismaHouse

Instagram.com/CharismaHouseBooks

SILOAM

(Health)

Pinterest.com/CharismaHouse

REALMS

(Fiction)

Facebook.com/RealmsFiction